I See Movies

in My Head

Phillip D. Reisner

ISBN: 978-1-4669-3736-9 (sc)
ISBN: 978-1-4669-3737-6 (e)

Trafford rev. 06/27/2012

 www.trafford.com

North America & international
toll-free: 1 888 232 4444 (USA & Canada)
phone: 250 383 6864 ◆ fax: 812 355 4082

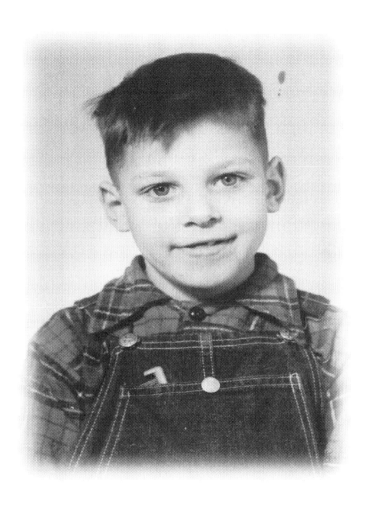

I wish I could go back in time with more than organic films in my head, and feel sweet, special and innocent again. I wish I could be six years old again, and ignorantly unique without worldly knowledge to clutter my heart, mind and soul.

PREFACE

In my earthly beginning, there was weak awareness and strong innocence. From egg and sperm, creation brought birth and growth, truth and wisdom, faith and spirituality. Out of living experience came collected memories, stowed like a sailor's worldly keepsakes. Maybe someone a whole lot smarter than me knows how it all works, this remembering thing, this collecting of knowledge process. For me, it is significantly storing these life souvenirs as movies in my head. I began documenting my early life with one still picture of a room, then sunshine passing through a window, then wind fluttering white curtains.

Of course, I did not know words, definitions or names at that time, but I soon made the correlation between pictures and words. I learned to read, observe and define my world. I then put these discovered abilities to work recalling motion pictures in my head.

As I recalled early visual pictures and films, I put words, definitions and names to them. I later defined while filming. I currently film in 3-D, Technicolor and surround sound. Oh, I have come far in this remembering thing, this collecting of knowledge thing.

I am not that sweet little boy pictured above. I do not see myself while looking at that picture. I have films of him living life, but it is difficult to turn the camera around and see myself. It is impossible for the eye to see itself unless looking into a mirror, or watching a film of itself. That little boy is another person in another time. I am a different person today after accumulating a lifetime of discovering self and learning how to fit into my unique universe. I have a million pictures and movies in my head depicting a baby, little boy and young man progressing towards wisdom and an inevitable ending of accumulation. It has been difficult to edit, select and limit which films to share with you.

Life is like learning how to run the four-hundred meter race in track. It is a balance between improving time and preserving energy, speeding up and not running out of energy.

I remember running that race and have several films of me having success and failure running the four-hundred yard race on cinder tracks. If I sped up too little, I had too much left at the end. If I sped up too much, I fell on my face. Life then is like life now, consisting of learning and adjusting, learning and adjusting, and I have much of it on film to prove my point.

I wish I could go back to those innocent times with more than movies in my head. I wish I could go back with more than acquired melancholy feelings and memories, and perhaps do many things differently. I know one thing I would do differently; I would tell my family "I love you" more.

Saying, "I love you" was a thing my family did not do back in the old days. I, however, never doubted their love for me. I hope my family never doubted my love for them. I just think it would have been a good thing to say it. I was twenty-something before I gave my dad a hug. I wish I had told him those three words, told him the words that I tell my wife, children and siblings today. Sometimes it is too late to say I love you. We should all practice saying and showing that we love each other, especially family members.

I believe that I came into the world innocent, as innocent as a blank sheet of paper, an empty computer, a newborn baby's brain. Like paper, computer and brain, the basic operating system is in place; it is just a matter of opening mind and being willing to receive information.

We gain knowledge and wisdom through experience. Knowledge and wisdom process within the brain and record in the mind. The soul then collects everything as if a suitcase for transporting to heaven by way of the Earth visiting spirit. I believe God will ask me to open my soul suitcase for inspection when I get to Heaven.

I can see my suitcase now. I am mentally filming the opening of it right now. I see pictures, composed books, film canisters, video tapes, CD disks. I see diplomas, certificates, report cards and evaluations. I see mementos, coins, watches and a gold ring. There is no bottom, no end to the provoking memorabilia present within my soul suitcase.

I am awe struck and all I can say when looking into my soul suitcase is, "Oh, my God."

The older I get the more details I film and now my mind is constantly filming and reflecting reality. I simply call up a picture, thought or feeling, and a projector starts clicking and a bright light begins streaming. I do not hear voices in my head, but my movies are not silent. I hear with my mind. I hear my father's deep voice giving advice and my sweet mother warning, both are concerned about my safety. Even though my movies are mostly silent, I somehow remember correlating spoken words. Dialogue is creeping into my movies these days, drawing attention and amplifying visual recordings.

I see bits and pieces of my soul collection. I see my original unimportance changing as I become important. I think that I am similar to a blank piece of paper coming to life through written words, but I am more like a complicated roll of celluloid coming to life through experienced illusion.

I faithfully believe that God brought Himself into the world through Jesus as a baby, with an innocent and blank mind of humanity. I ask, how else could He show unimportance and importance of each human being other than through a baby? Jesus was God on Earth. We are tiny pieces of God on Earth ourselves. We can only pray to be a little Christ-like.

Jesus was born innocent, learned how to be a human, suffer like a human, die like a human. He was not completely human, as we are not completely human, but spiritual beings incased in a human body.

We begin blank and innocent, designed to grow into a human being for as long as we have time on Earth. God puts the operating system in our DNA. God places it in every cell. We wait for booting like a computer. Soon we become self-aware and the human experience begins. I do not know how many people are capable of filming their lives, but it is a joy for me. It is a tool for remembering, learning and teaching.

I believe that my life will end with a strong awareness of self and an observation of God's hand. He will be reaching to help me up from my knees for my soul suitcase will be very heavy. I pray He will be pleased when I open it. I pray He will smile.

CONTENTS

INTRODUCTION

There are millions of pictures and movies in my head, mind and soul. I use my collective essence for planning, problem solving and recollecting experiences. Personal films help construct my beliefs, philosophy and spirituality. I can nearly see the way back to heaven. I think many of my spiritual beliefs come from existing knowledge gained from other than Earth.

I see my spiritual world and God's universe in terms of simple wisdom. I think the Bible goes over and over the important things, throughout saying nearly the same thing. It says, love God more than anything or anyone else, treat everyone with God's love and believe that Jesus is the way to get back home. If you are a Christian, then Jesus is your ticket on the light speed train to heaven. Of course, it is simple, but not easy and everything has to be honest, true and from the heart. Maybe there are several ways to get to heaven; however, if you are a Christian, there is only one-way, that being through Jesus Christ.

I see these movies in my head by calling them up through subject area thought and then visualization. An image appears and, near instantly, moving pictures create a movie. I can nearly smell and taste the popcorn of life. I amaze myself sometimes concerning recalling names, places and people. I seem to have a horrible real time conscious memory concerning names, but my subconscious films reveal more than I ever expect.

If you will venture into the past with me, I shall try to conjure up some of the movies that come to mind concerning my childhood and early adulthood. I hope what I have to show you with words will be worth your while. I wish you could see the movies that I see in my head.

Chapter I

Sunday	Monday	Tuesday	Wednesday	Thursday	Friday	Saturday
					1	2
3	4	5	6	7	8	9
10	11 Veterans Day	12	13	14	15	16
17	18	19	20	21	22	23
24	25	26	27	28	29	30

www.PrintableCalendar.com

Beginning Awareness

1

Oh sweet,
"Innocence,"
you're like an
angel bringing
me to Earth on a
strand of
heavenly light.

I repose with
your protection in
warm pure security
earthly while.

Provocateur

Life is a
provocateur,
pushing, prodding,
probing and
nudging.
Life is a bastard,
lying, cheating,
raping and
killing.
Life is a lover,
kissing, hugging,
sweet-talking and
love making.

o

I experience
what life
inexplicably
offers through
more than a
million
good, bad and
indifferent
stories, scenes and
character actors.

I recall too
much and
not enough at
prompted times.
Life teaches a
thousand lessons,

some haunt and
others pacify as
movies in my head.
They seek my soul and
wash my mind, and
will not fade.
An ever expanding
knowledge tree
involuntarily grows
in my mind,
overtly providing
spiritual fruit.

Oh how well,
omnipotent God,
you kindly created me,
joining egg and
sperm, crafting boy
into man, and yet
not allowing all
innocence to die.
A touch of purity
remains within as
I naively seek
preservation for a
hundred years.

Innocence

Oh sweet,
"Innocence,"
you're like an
angel bringing
me to Earth on a
strand of
heavenly light.
I repose with
your protection in
warm pure security
earthly while.
Some are
doomed,
thrashing in
impurity,
seeking salvation
even before earthly
life begins.

I, however,
swim to earth in
unknown liquid
time and space
blessed womb,
innocent,
unaware and
immature for
fifty-eight days.

Body then accepts
spirit while
growing aware of
true self;

thus a
chipping away at
innocence begins.

Look now into
my blue eyes and
see humanity
gazing.
Look at
my clear face and
see no wrinkled
distress.
Look at
my smile as
emerging grace.

I see myself in
retrospect as a
soul bits and
pieces collector,
knowing self by
knowledge and
wisdom hoard,
knowing self by
pictures and movies
reward collected.

Sunlight and Yellow Walls

I crib lay in a small
yellow painted room,
crying and fussing with colic.
Bright sunlight streams
through a six lighted window,
through white curtains and
into my absorbing mind.

My mother, Mary Louise,
holds and cuddles me,
feeds and bathes me.
I feel my face against
her warm soft breast.

I don't blame her for
my crying and silent pain.
I'm not angry or distressed.
I accept subtle fate and
define loud discomfort.
I see truth and gain
confidence through what
I mind movie record.

My House

I see a small two bedroom house where I first two years of life reside in Terre Haute, Indiana.

It is small elevation situated beyond a concrete wall holding back soil from sidewalk and street.

It corner lot sits, front door facing westward dusk, my yellow back bedroom faces eastward dawn.

It's too small for a facade, only a small stoop protects a heavy, strangely oversized, green door.

It has small green painted window frames placed side by side to allow abundant sunlight.

I see my room with all its yellow grace and warmth, comforting my replanted spirit and soul.

I see my house sitting on a small hill as if a spacious castle with a concrete wall protecting.

I gather my senses, stow my thoughts and begin to recognize a changing world in which I live.

I innocently stand looking at home security while recalling mother's strong hand touching my soul.

o

I saw that house many years later,
but now it is gone, torn down,
put to rest like my parents
who within began a marriage.

Best Friends

Charlotte Dowling
is a friend of
my mother
who city lives.
Her husband
translates music.

She baby-sits
me while
my mother helps
my dad
transport goods
during day time.

I don't nap
well and
find myself
laying in bed,
trying to sleep at
Charlotte's house.

Swirling dark
red patterned
wallpaper,
stares back at
me for
seemingly hours.

I faintly mind see
my mother and
Charlotte laughing.
It's a short silent movie
mentally confirming
their existence.

I can nearly
mind see them
standing outside,
side by side in
bright sunlight
in nineteen forty-two.

Mother is a
city girl at
heart, but will
become a
farmer's wife and
never look back.

o

Charlotte and
my mother,
Louise, remained
best friends for
years even after
mother moved to
Farmersburg and
Charlotte to Valdosta.

Metal Parrot

Mother carries me awhile.
I then walk towards a
small local grocery store.
I am less than two, yet
beginning to realize a
world of intrigue is
opening before
my innocent eyes.

I see a bright red and
yellow metal parrot sign
advertising bread,
fastened to a screen door.
It belongs to a small red brick
corner building with an
angular exterior wall.
It swings outward and a
heavy white door swings inward.
A small brass bell tinkles as
we maneuver through doors and
past silent parrot sign hanging.

Now homeward we walk
two blocks from that grocery store.
I'm learning my way from
yellow bedroom to yellow parrot.
I am small as is my world.
Life strangely continues to
silently accumulate in my head.

Lovelace

They call my dad,
"Pappy," but I'll not
call him Pappy or
even Pop for it
seems disrespectful.

Bill and Manard
Niemeyer dream of
Lovelace Trucking.
They've driven trucks
since thirty-nine.

They start Lovelace
in forty-two and ask
my dad to be a partner.
Bill says, "It means eating
beans for several years."

I hear my dad say,
"No thanks,"
thinking family first and
own decisions have
shared consequences.

Last Semi Truck

I faintly see my dad's last
semi truck, street sitting
in nineteen forty-four.

I clearly see hood, grill and
bumper, then mind shift to
side and running board.

It looks Dodge like,
nearly new, nineteen forty-three,
highway freedom bound.

It pulls what looks to be an
eighteen foot trailer seeking
stacked and fitted cargo.

Father lifts my sister onto a
fender as someone
takes pictures beside me.

It's a lifetime love transition for
trucks have taken my dad
far and wide on evolving highways.

Here in my ever expanding
theater mind I miraculously record
life evolving when three years old.

Reason

My dad
quit driving
trucks full-time
because of
eye problems,
poor eyesight or
nearly going blind,
I know not reason.

He now
wears thin
silver rimmed
glasses and
I see small dents
on his nose where
they rest after
removing them.

He quit
driving trucks,
became a
farmer and
moved from
town, and
I'm glad
he changed.

Chapter II

DECEMBER 1944

Sunday	Monday	Tuesday	Wednesday	Thursday	Friday	Saturday
					1	2
3	4	5	6	7	8	9
10 Hanukkah begins at sunset	11	12	13	14	15	16
17	18	19	20	21	22	23
24	25 Christmas	26	27	28	29	30
31						

www.PocketCalendar.com

Seeing Reality

I explore old barn,
chicken coop and
apple trees, but not
inviting muddy pond.

I enjoy tall grass
beneath feet and
seek precious hiding
four-leaf clovers.

My New Home

We are moving from
Terre Haute to a
small farm
near Pimento,
Indiana today.
It is a nice place
located west of
town, but
I kind of dislike
leaving my little
white castle
on a hill.

My new home
located on a
few acres of
good farm land
seeks my attention.
I don't know where
my father got
money enough to
start farming.
I suspect from
selling his two
semi trucks.

o

I see a
dining room,
kitchen and
living room.
I see and

feel cold air
on my feet
from a furnace
cold air return.
I gaze outside
through large
windows.

My house is a
one and a half story
modern structure.
My upper level
room is across
from a bathroom.
I further gaze,
noticing a large
living area and
begin creating
mental images to
last a lifetime.

o

I could drive directly to that
once new house right now.
I wonder if it yet stands.
I see it farmland sitting with
evergreen trees out front.
I wonder if those trees yet stand.
I see its basic floor plan and
where I nightly slept, and
where one night Santa appeared.
I wonder if Santa yet there exists.

Allis Chalmers

I faintly hear an old noisy projector
mechanically feeding mental pictures
through my head, creating moving images
born a long time ago, yet as if yesterday.

o

I see my father's
first tractor, a used orange
Allis Chalmers, driveway sitting.

I picture my sister
standing on a front tractor
extension in her winter coat.

I strike and cut her head with a
generator pulley from that old
Allis tractor when four years old.

It has metal fins for cooling and a
v-shape for a belt, and is conveniently
ground laying, replaced by a new one.

It becomes a weapon for an
immature mind guided hand
wishing no harm, yet foolishly strikes.

Guilt seeps as Mother reprimands,
asking why I did such a thing, but
I have no answer and no remedy.

Little Brown Turd

Several women stand around talking,
eating cake and drinking coffee.
They're attending an adult
Home Economics meeting at
my future school building.

I and another little boy are
only there because
we're four years old and have
no baby-sitter while our mothers
learn about being economical.

I am wearing loose fitting overalls,
brown shoes and a blue striped shirt.
I have to poop and cannot get
my mother's attention.
She is preoccupied, too busy.

I try holding it, but cannot and
finally let go, lacking knowledge
on how to handle my situation.
A little brown turd drops from
my pants onto shiny wooden flooring.

I move and hide behind Mother's skirt.
I hear a woman ask, "What is that?"
Another asks with greater emphasis,
bending to inspect, "What is that?"
Of course, I know what "that" is.

They soon figure it out as I pretend to
know nothing and be not responsible.
No one speaks of it again while

Mother removes it with paper towel,
then privately cleans me with toilet paper.

I am relieved that no one wants to
punish me, make me feel like a fool.
I am embarrassed enough.
I need no learning lessons.
I teach myself many things

o

I remember pooping
my pants again when
in first grade and
Doug Ring was restroom
sent to help clean me.
He never forgot or
forgave me for that
teacher ordered duty.
I am yet embarrassed
in own obtuse film way.

Santa

I am sure in
my childish
mind that
I indeed see
Santa.
It is not
Father for in
grasping mind
I faintly see
Santa in all
his glory:
red coat,
white beard,
big toy bag.
I run
back to bed,
pulling covers
over head and
play vivid images
in my mind,
seeing Santa
clearly.
I remain in bed,
not wanting to
scare him away,
finally going to sleep,
thinking about
tomorrow and
seeing wonderful
future images.

Fantasy

My mind
wanders
farther than into
sky and
clouds where
everyone knows
my name.
I wish to
remain or at
least soon
return to
fantasy.
I hope to
never exhaust
my daydreaming
mind.
I hope
no one steals
my flying
inattention.
It is soaring
creativity that allows
growing up well.
Truth and
reality haunt.
Imagination and
fantasy obsess.
I fly high through
blue sky, through
clouds and
sunshine alike.
I am happy.

Organic Pictures

I engage organic
moving pictures
in my earthly
head.

Someday
film maker and
theater will become
totally organic.

My movies shall
be spiritual gems
preserved in
acquiring soul.

Innocence seeps
like light through
collecting
mind's eye.

I believe
movie making
will be forever, but
time says no.

Repeatedly

First time in life
I have venture room.
Country living suits me
without streets and cars.

I have sixty
roaming acres, but am
only five and have rules,
self preservation rules.

I explore old barn,
chicken coop and
apple trees, but not
inviting muddy pond.

I enjoy tall grass
beneath feet and
seek precious hiding
four-leaf clovers.

I climb, run and
jump with a small
log chain hanging from
my sturdy neck.

I front porch sit,
watching few cars pass,
seeing dust rise, float and
fall like magical clouds.

Rain, lightning and
thunder wash everything.
Life is like dust and
experience like rain.

I am unknowingly a
film maker,
theater operator and
mind proofing self.

My world is
changing before
sensing eyes and
in recording mind.

Sweet innocence
holds my hand
while guilt and shame
tap my shoulder.

I don't suspect that
green grass and
four-leaf clovers are
disappearing.

I fear life is only a
now illusion that I'm
documenting for
future reality gazing.

o

*I remember my dad
reinforcing not going to
our pond by catching a
huge snapping turtle
from it and making
turtle soup out of him.*

Chapter III

JANUARY 1946

Sunday	Monday	Tuesday	Wednesday	Thursday	Friday	Saturday
		1 New Years Day	2	3	4	5
6	7	8	9	10	11	12
13	14	15	16	17	18	19
20	21	22	23	24	25	26
27	28	29	30	31		

www.PocketCalendar.com

Provoking
Integrity

I reluctantly leave
my second home as if
I have a choice at
six years old and

move five miles south,
locating in
Vigo County, but
bordering Sullivan.

Pocket Knife

I stand before
Al Vandyke with
Father behind me,
confessing that
I am a thief.
I took a
pocketknife from a
display case
three days ago and
now wish to admit
faulty thinking.

I return it,
ready to receive
punishment.
My father and
I have
talked and
decided to
do right.

My ears are
burning,
stomach is
churning and
I can barely
speak requesting
forgiveness words.

Al, also known as
Fluffy,
because of his
array of hair,

lets me off with
two store
cleaning hours
punishment.
I am relieved,
Fluffy, is happy and
my father is
pleased with
my confession.

I fear
it will not be
my last desire to
steal, but for now,
I have discipline.
I ask,
"Will I always
have discipline?
Will my father always
help me out of
trouble?"

I fear
growing up will
come slowly and
not easily.
I fear honesty
will test me and
I will ask
more than once,
"Will you forgive me?"
I feel it is not
so natural and
most people,
not just little boys,
struggle with
honesty.

I frequently hear
Father's deep
voice speaking,
teaching and
soliciting answers.
Many memories
fade, but mind
movies endure.

.

My father's
image and
voice remain
inside my head
even when
he's not present.
It keeps me
well advised.

Peanuts and Coke

I'm tagging
along with
my dad today,
"my shadow,"
he calls me.
With pride and
admiration,
I walk beside
him into a
local gas station to
drink pop and
eat peanuts.
I enjoy
tagging along and
probably will until
old enough to
make own
noticeable shadow.
After that,
I'll work with,
stand by and
walk beside, but
I suspect
I shall always be
his shadow.
It's great to
drink pop
instead of
water, ice tea or
lemon-aide.
Soda pop is a
luxury to me.
I always follow

same procedure:
drink some Coke,
pour peanuts into
pop bottle and
then same time
eat and drink.

9:00 P.M. Tuesday, July 2, 1946

There are back room
slot machines, but
I'm not allowed to
play them.
Station owner,
Hap, also
pays-off on
pinball machines
placed out front.

My dad is
very big and
strong;
slot machines
are heavy.
Sometimes Hap
calls my dad on
our crank wall phone,
asking him to
slot machine carry to a
secluded cabin
located out back
near property edge.
He says,
"Excise men are
coming to raid.
I've been
tipped off."

He has to
get his machines
out of sight
right away.

I wait tonight in
darkness while
my dad and
Hap move
slot machines.
I want to help.
I feel big
enough to help,
just not
old enough to help
I guess.

8:00 A.M. Wednesday, July 9, 1946

Hap's small
gas station is
rather dark and
cluttered.
It's standing room
only except near a
large brass
cash register
where two metal
stools sit,
placed for
eating and
loitering.
Most men,
just stand around
in a small space.
I don't
understand

most of what
my dad and
his friends
talk about, and
when old enough to
understand,
I suspect I'll seldom
come here.

Product hangs
overhead and
on walls.
Product lays
on wall shelves,
counters and
metal shelf units.
Two large
pop machines
sit near pathway end.
My peanuts
clip hang on a
metal display unit,
along with bags of
potatoes chips and
cheese puffs.
I like
cheese puffs, but
always chose
peanuts.

A mechanic's
bay and
tire repair area
rest beyond a
large doorway.
Scattered tools
on metal

bench tops with
two large vises,
one for clamping,
another for
pipe fitting,
wait use.
A red and
silver rolling
tool chest with
drawers half open
also awaits
Hap's attention.
Hap, however,
seldom leaves
his well padded
counter stool.
Whole mechanical
area smells of
new tires and
grease with
gas vapors
combining them.
It's a
strong odor and
I'm glad adjoining
door is closed.
It overwhelms
coke and peanut
delicacy odor.

9:00 A.M. Tuesday, October 15, 1946

Today pinball and
slot machines
noisily roll.
Men talk and
Hap laughs.

I'm eating
peanuts and
drinking pop.
My dad looks and
smiles at me.
All is right
in my world.

o

It's strange how
security spoke with a
father's smile, a
handful of nuts and a
few coke swallows.
It's strange how a
shadow can exist
long after cause and
effect is gone, and
only film survives.

Cracklins

Dad and I
frequently go to
Roy Week's
slaughterhouse.
It's just a few
miles from
our farm.
Local men
sit around a
warm pot belly
stove there
during winter,
eating "cracklins,"
also known as
pork rinds.
These, however, are
different from
store bought,
they're thick and
authentic.
Roy makes them from
hog skin and
fat somehow,
I think they're also
called "fatback."
They are
delicious, but for
some a
bit repulsive.

It seems a
strange place to
hang out, but

it's warm and
intimate inside Roy's
murderous
slaughterhouse.
It has a
distinct odor that's
pleasantly soft and
warm to my nose,
brain and mind.
Death's
specter lurks
behind a wall,
beyond my view.
Death is a faint
concept for me, but an
approaching reality.
I don't understand
life or death fully.
It's all around me,
seeming almost natural
on a farm.

9:00 AM Wednesday, December 11, 1946

I step beyond that
ominous wall and
see a long runway
leading towards a
wide slaughterhouse door.
I see a steer being
up ramp pushed and
shot between his eyes
just after passing
door threshold.
He crumples like a
black water bag with
red blood seeping.

He is motionless
on a slick floor,
absorbing blood.

I look away,
turning towards
warm fire and
my safe potbelly stove
sitting place.
I soon realize
it is our steer
who took that last
short walk
towards heaven.
I will later eat
his muscle and
stolen strength with
little conscience or shame.
Some lessons are simple,
almost natural, and
I learn that
life is fragile and
guilt is flimsy.

I sit at home,
playing movies
in my head,
remembering
rifle sound and
red blood gushing.
It's a bit
disconcerting.

Roy's daughter never
slaughterhouse
appears,
riding her horse instead,

just beyond ear shot.
I want to
ride her horse
instead of
stove sitting and
cracklin eating.
I want to be beyond
ear shot of a
lot of things
going on around me.
Death innocence will
fade with each
eaten steer mouthful.
Time and distance from
Roy's slaughterhouse will
cause less
conscience fraying.
I sense that
reality is every day
into mind seeping and
I have no defense
against it.

Importance

I am
beginning to
believe a man's
humility and
importance
emerges as a
boy recognizes
own fate.

They hide
beneath a
mother's
expectations and
flourish
beyond a
father's
anticipation.

I fear
I'll not
listen to
either parent and
not grasp or
understand
illusive humility or
importance.

o

*My learned lessons and
gained wisdom did not fall on
deaf mind or hardened heart.*

Big Farm House

I reluctantly leave
my second home, as if
I have a choice at
six years old, and
move five miles south,
locating in
Vigo County, but
bordering Sullivan.
It is a big white
farmhouse with
ten rooms and a
huge screened porch.

Porch runs nearly
full house length.
My dad and
I are sitting during a
late spring storm,
watching rain and
lightening, and
listening to thunder.
We stay placed until a
million electrical volts
boom and flash,
traveling down a
lightning ground wire
five feet before our eyes.

3:30 P.M. Thursday, June 12, 1947

Charlie

I watch
Charlie Vangilder
magically transform
two-thirds of
our screened porch
into bathroom and
utility room.
He spends much time
pulling up his
too big pants.
Maybe his belt is
too loose to
support tools
carried in pockets.

It irritates
my mother,
watching him
constantly
pulling up
his trousers.
She is
calculating costly
trouser pulling time.

Charlie is a
good carpenter and
good man, but
what do I know,
I'm only six years old.
I'm learning much,
watching him
work with precision and

grace.
He's much like
my father,
truthful, confident and
skillful.
They both like
working constantly,
ingeniously
constructing with
firm callused
mind and
hands,
seeking little reward.
I'm beginning to
figure out that
labor's plight is
forever in
working hands.
Time's plight is
forever in
calculating minds.

Running Water

Heat is great, but
having inside
running water and a
bathroom is wonderful.

I have a bathroom,
not a furnace, but
my middle
upstairs room
stays warm from a
floor vent above a
first floor stove.

Venita's south
end room is
cold with
door closed to
hide secret things.
She requires
sister privacy.

Heat is great, but
having inside
running water and a
bathroom is wonderful.

o

*Thanks to
Charlie Vangilder,
we obtained both
running water and a
bathroom.*

Chapter IV

Sunday	Monday	Tuesday	Wednesday	Thursday	Friday	Saturday
					1	2
3	4	5	6	7	8	9
10	11	12	13	14	15	16
17	18	19	20	21	22	23
24	25	26	27	28	29	30
31						

Saving Life

Mr. Stewart
does well in business,
lives in a nice
big brick house with
tall white painted pillars.

It even has a
driveway portico
side entrance.
I bet it has
twenty rooms.

Mrs. Moore

I don't like
my first school day,
being unhappy,
feeling boxed in.
I leave school,
about ten o-clock,
planning to walk home.
It's two miles and
I know my way.
I can mind
see it well.

I head west, but a
man stops me at
school grounds' edge and
escorts me back to
Mrs. Moore,
my first grade
teacher.
I tell her,
"It's just
too damn hot to
be in school."

I think Mrs. Moore
agrees with me, but
cannot say so directly.
She talks me
into staying and
things go smoothly
from that time on.
Mrs. Moore is a
gentle woman.

She's like an
angel to me at
age six,
needing love when
away from
my sweet mother.

She's a
great teacher,
teaching me
many things a
first grader
should know.
She extends
much of what
I've already
learned at home.
I think that
I love
Mrs. Moore.
She is like
family to me.

Barbershop

Paul Chris is short,
fat and friendly.
He sits on a
sagging stool
attached to a sturdy
barber chair.
He is constantly
shifting his weight
on a red plastic seat,
riding it like a
bucking horse,
chance
slipping off.

There are big
humming fans,
thirty inches in diameter,
placed on pedestals,
stirring air on a
hot late summer day.
They have a
unique Paul Chris
barbershop sound.

I clearly see
my dark brown hair
falling onto a
white tile floor.
Sunshine flows
through large
plate glass windows
facing west.
Outside noise is

drowned out from
people talking,
fans humming and
clippers purring in
my ears.
.
We have a
local barbershop
in Farmersburg,
I go there
most times, but
Paul's big city
six chair shop is exciting.
Men's magazines
concerning women
wearing skimpy
underwear are
scattered about.
I glance at them,
then look closer, but
my dad says
I'm too young.
I know there are
more revealing
magazines out there.
I'll check them out
later in life.
A few years
make a difference in
what is available.
All I know is
something powerful
stirs inside while
looking at
half-naked women
pictures.
I see those magazines

when home in
movie playing mind and
touch myself, and
it feels good.

We quit going there
after Paul died of a
heart attack at
forty-three.
I remember
my dad remarking,
"Paul was so young, but
he weighed over
three hundred
pounds."
I yet have little
understanding of
life and death.
I think
my dad is a
little bit old, but
I don't see him
dying any time soon.

My parents never
act old or give
impression of
feeling old.
I think my dad
would certainly
be young if
he died today.

o

My dad had a
heart attack a

few months later while
harvesting soybeans.
He started feeling
pain about noon,
complained much at
dinner time and was
hospitalized at
ten o-clock at night,
but he didn't die
like Paul Chris.

o

It's a
pleasant movie
I play of myself,
my dad and
Paul Chris
in that big city
barbershop.
I'm young and
innocent
straight off a
small farm, but
I well know that
I will grown-up,
playing those movies
in my head,
realizing innocence is
slowly being
chipped away.
Personal history is
coming alive at
my casual request.
I'm already aware of
my movie making gift.

Big Shoe's BBQ

My dad is a
raccoon hunter and
sometimes
takes raccoons,
next day after killed,
to a black man
named, "Big Shoe,"
who lives in
Terre Haute.

He owns a
part-time
BBQ place called
"Big Shoe's BBQ."
Big Shoe actually
works at a
junk yard, but
BBQing is
his passion and
sideline business.

I see his
successful
county fair
BBQ tent.
I wonder if
possibly some
raccoon meat is
between
my sandwich bun.

Big Shoe is a
large man like my dad.

I faintly see them
standing together, a
formidable twosome of
distinct men.

o

*I think my dad was
prejudiced, but when
I asked about
Big Shoe, about
him being a negro,
he only said,
"Big Shoe is
my friend."
Maybe he wasn't
prejudiced, but
used that one
prejudiced "n" word
occasionally.
He honestly didn't
see Big Shoe as a
black man,
just a man,
just a friend.*

o

I only know
one black man, and
that is Big Shoe.
I don't think
about black and
white.
I just know
Big Shoe is
my dad's friend,

thus a friend of
mine.

I sense at
six years old that
nothing will
ever change.
Life is perfect, but
there is talk about
racial change at
Paul's barbershop,
Roy's slaughterhouse and
Big Shoe's scrap yard.
I understand
little about it.
I'm colorblind and
don't know it.
I'm ignorant
about much and
know it.
Maybe some
ignorance is a
good thing.

Granary

A white painted
granary door is
wide open.
It's dark inside,
like a silent cave.
Weevil have infested
our stored wheat.
My father douses
bug killer while
knee deep in
golden wheat.
He moves slowly,
wading wheat with a
five-gallon
deadly concoction
container spewing
white poison.

A stinky
odor floats past
open door,
burns nose and
waters eyes.
I retreat, but
soon Father
anxiously calls,
"Help me, son."
I look inside,
seeing him
trying to escape,
wading through
tainted wheat.
Colorless

asphyxiating odor
overcomes him
like a colorless
evil spirit consuming.
He cannot crawl out.
I thoughtlessly
wade inside,
holding breath,
wheat hip deep.
I struggle to pull him,
straining and
grabbing
his overall straps.
He attempts to
help, but has
little strength.
I struggle,
heart pounding as
lungs beg for air,
beg breathing.
I miraculously pull
him over threshold
onto ground.

Father is still
except for
shallow breathing,
nearly unconscious.
He moves slightly and
finally props himself
against an outside wall.
I watch him
literally come
back to life.
His eyes open.
"Thank you, son,"
he whispers.

I feel unfamiliar
heart relief as
mind and
soul are suddenly
different.
I am different.
I run to Mother,
seeking another's
help for
I know not
what else to do.
I'm just a kid
who witnessed
near father death.
I mumble a few
Oregon Baptist
Church words with
ignorant conviction, then
louder I say,
"Thank you, God."

Frozen Eggs

Henry Stewart
owned an
International Harvester
farm implement
dealership.
My dad
purchased Farmall
tractors and
associated
equipment from him.

o

My dad is
walking among
shiny red tractors
placed on a shiny
showroom floor.
I follow with
my shiny smiling face.
He is talking to
Mr. Stewart about
farm equipment.
Mr. Stewart
does well in business,
lives in a nice
big brick house with
tall white painted pillars.
It even has a
driveway portico
side entrance.
I bet it has
twenty rooms.

He has a monopoly on
farm equipment sales and
service around here,
no competition for miles.

His business is near
railroad tracks,
same ones as
behind my house.
A train slowly passes
through town,
making plate glass
windows rattle.
I love trains,
watching them is a
pastime of mine.
Year after year,
I watch
railroad engines
evolve from
steam to diesel.
I see it all with
my eyes and
place it all
in my head;
old engines
stop for water
while new diesels
pass an old charitable
obsolete water tower.

Mr. Stewart and
my dad are
shaking hands
just before we leave.
I bet my dad
just bought a

new tractor.
It's probably that
new shiny red
Farmall H,
he has been
talking about lately.

9:15 A.M. Wednesday, June 17, 1948

I faintly hear
Mr. Stewart
seriously talking to
my dad about
Futures investing;
he already knows
my dad only invests
in hard work.
I think Mr. Stewart
makes a lot of
money in Futures.
He probably also
makes a lot of
money selling
farm equipment to
my dad.
He's talking about a
train carload of
frozen eggs that
he's buying and
will sell to someone
for a new thing
called a cake mix.
He says
it doesn't matter
if they're frozen.
I bet Mother will
buy some cake mixes.

Making cakes is a
lot of work.
It sounds good,
makes sense to
me, but not to
my dad.
He says,
"I don't gamble," yet
every season of
every year
he gambles on weather,
time and prices.
He is telling
Mr. Stewart that
he will stick with
farming and
trucking, not Futures.

Riding Ponies

I ride my
Shetland ponies
everywhere, to
near pastures and
far farm ends,
seeking adventure
mostly as if a cowboy.
I eat beans from a
metal plate with a
wooden spoon.
I nap on a
sleeping roll with
head on saddle at
far pasture edge.
I spend time
pretending,
imagining and
dreaming.

My dad sells many of
our ponies at
one time or another.
It's a business for
him, but a
pleasure for me.
Many ponies are
with us long enough for
loving attachment.
A few pony years is a
big chunk of life to me.
It's a short
working relationship to
my dad.

10:00 A.M. Sunday, July 11, 1948

I mentally record
my best ever pony,
"King,"
who is presently
our stud and
my best farm friend.
Dad keeps
newborn fillies,
sells horse colts and
trains selected mares.
He is getting a
new stud today
because after a
few years,
they inbreed.

We have
twenty mares and
one stud.
Today my dad is also
selling King to a
boy who lives in
Farmersburg.
I'll never forget
King and
our fun times.

10:00 A.M. Wednesday, July 18, 1948

I mentally shoot
another film,
seeing King as
we drive past
his new home while in
my dad's black

forty-nine Ford
pickup truck.
King's name is
white painted on every
opened wooden
window shutter of
his new home barn.

I believe that boy
loves King as
much as I do.
I have a mare
replacement for him,
but really, there's
no replacement for
King.

10:00 A.M. Friday, August 13, 1948

I cannot remember
many other pony names
except Minnie,
Mitsie and Patsy.
My dad started with
Minnie and Mitsie,
developing a herd of
Shetland ponies
from those two and a
stud whose name
I forget.

Patsy was a favorite of
his because
she same birthed a
paint offspring
every year.
Dad keeps most

fillies and trains
them to
work as a team
under harness.
He makes
wagons and
carts for
riding, and
leather straps for
pulling logs.

Shetland ponies were
used in coal mines a
long time ago,
they are small, but
mighty strong.

10:00 A.M. Monday, August 23, 1948

I am in a lush
twelve acre pasture,
playing cowboy,
riding here and
there with
camping supplies.

I stop to eat lunch
under a tree
near a far fence,
tying my pony to a
fence post.
I finish eating a
sandwich and
tie a near empty
metal lunch pail to
my saddle;
it makes a

metal to metal
rattling sound.

My surprised pony
jumps to one side,
causing a
louder rattle that
scares her more.
She begins to run,
pulling reins from
fence post and
then out of my hands as
rattling gets
constantly louder.
I try to
catch her to
no avail.
She runs
faster and
will not stop,
running and
running.
She is
lathered and
tired, but
will not stop;
rattling
will not cease.

She slows,
nearly collapsing,
finally stopping
near me.
I feel horrible.
She could have
injured or killed
herself and

it would have been
my fault.
I must replace
her ignorance with
my intelligence and
accept responsibility.

o

I slowly learned
about responsibility,
sometimes easily,
sometimes difficultly, and
sometimes at others'
unfortunate expense.

10:00 A.M. Monday, May 17, 1948

Smoking

My father smoked cigarettes.
I watched him inhale and exhale smoke.
He gracefully manipulated those white tobacco sticks.
It looked fun, interesting and cool.

o

I steal cigarettes from a desk drawer.
I try smoking a cigarette in our big barn.
I choke and cough for a long time.
I press onward and finally get sick.

3:00 P.M. Saturday, July 10, 1948

Father catches me smoking.
We talk about burning barns.
He doesn't say smoking is wrong.
He only says don't do it.

3:00 P.M. Saturday, July 31, 1948

I need more reasoning.
I need more facts.
I need my ass kicked.
Father finally satisfies my needs.

Uncle Art

Uncle Art silently sits beside me
on a homemade wooden bench
in warm summer sunlight.
He's a retired train engineer and
married to my Aunt Artha.
He smells like fresh laundry soap,
dressed in his newly washed and
starched pinstriped overalls.
He's wearing a starched blue denim shirt,
finely polished black high top shoes and a
starched pinstriped railroad man's hat.
Pride's in his eyes and trains are in his soul.
He gets dressed every day as if yet an engineer,
waiting for a call to drive trains again.
He's starting to build his own saw mill.
I think "no trains" reality is setting in.
Aunt Artha fixes orange Kool-aid and
mixes it with RC cola for me to drink.
It's a luxury I never get at home and a
strange mixture I only drink here
during my one week summer visit.
She makes her own lye soap and
teaches me how to systematically
wash myself, face first and butt last.
She's a good German woman.
No one teaches order like Aunt Artha.
She's devoting her life to serving
my grandparents and retired
engineer/saw mill operator Uncle Art.

Chapter V

SEPTEMBER 1948

Sunday	Monday	Tuesday	Wednesday	Thursday	Friday	Saturday
			1	2	3	4
5	6 Labor Day	7	8	9	10	11
12	13	14	15	16	17	18
19	20	21	22	23	24	25
26	27	28	29	30		

www.PrintableCalendar.com

Seeking
Truth

They say these are
His words, but
I can't read or
understand them.

I need simple
explanations to
complicated questions.

Mrs. Clary

I see Mrs. Clary's
second grade room
windows from outside.
I am late for
school.
I climb worn
wooden steps,
walk across a
polished floor and
pass into a
dim coat closet.
I hang
my lightweight
fall coat on a
metal wall hanger, then
pass through a
doorway and
enter Mrs. Clary's
bright classroom.
Classmates are
semi-circular sitting in
our reading area.
Everything stops,
silence prevails while
I find an empty chair.
Mrs. Clary is
sitting straight and
proper at center with
book in hand.
She immediately asks
me to read,
beginning at
page three top.

I am not ready to
read.
I am confused and
scramble for page
three.
My ears are hot and
I can barely think.

"Read,"
she commands.
I search for
page three.
I find it.
"Read,"
she orders again.
"Start at the beginning,"
I look at a blurry page,
I see words, but
cannot think or
mouth them.
I am thoughtless,
speechless.
"What happened to you?
It rained last night.
Did your little jewels
get rusty?
Read."
I cannot reason.
My mind is a blank.
I cannot remember
any words.

"The," a girl
next to me whispers.
I say, "The."
"Read,"
Mrs. Clary shouts.

"Man," my friend
again whispers.
"Quiet, Saundra."
Clary barks.
I say, "Man," but
cannot read a
third word.
"Oh, go to the
cloak room and
get out of my sight.
Your little jewels are
rusty."
Mrs. Clary says
while standing and
pointing.
I'm afraid she's
going to get that
big ruler out and
smack my hands, but
she doesn't,
just points.

8:15 A.M. Monday, September, 6 1948

I walk past
her big green
Boston fern
next to a window,
sucking up sunlight
like crazy.
I want to throw it
out one of those
big windows
along with Mrs. Clary.
Instead,
I cloak room head,
put my coat on and

walk out of school.
I'm in trouble and
have been in school
only five minutes.

8:25 A.M. Monday, September 6, 1948

I am next
speaking with
principal Ader,
explaining why
I walked outside and
went to recess early.
He finally lets
me off with a
reprimand.
I think
he understands
Mrs. Clary's
teaching methods.
It isn't soft and
gentle like
Mrs. Moore's approach,
that's for sure.

I think about
throwing Mrs. Clary
out a window
during lunch and
noon recess.
I nearly see
her flying from that
second story
window,
heading towards that
big green Boston fern,
previously thrown.

I finish lunch and
walk past a little
snack area within
our school basement,
just outside a
cafeteria door.
They sell
cinnamon balls to
my sweet liking.
I nickel buy three,
put in pocket and
sneak for an hour or
so during class.
They are sugar
coated and hot.
They scratch
mouth roof until
smooth from sucking.
I love them and
wish I could
afford twenty.
I feel better now with a
little comfort food.

o

I contracted an aversion to
reading from that moment on.
I cannot read well aloud yet today.
I clearly see mental movies of
Mrs. Clary, hear her voice and
feel damage done when recalling being
alone at night in my faintly lit bedroom.

Hundred Dollar Bill

It's mid morning and
I'm at recess,
running and
playing within a
green bush fence that
surrounds my elementary
school playground.
I take time out to
show my friends a
hundred and a
twenty dollar bill.
My parents
keep cash in a
desk drawer.
I've never before
seen a hundred
dollar bill and
neither has
Dennis and Paul.
Twenties are cool,
but hundreds are
awesome.
My pals are
impressed.
We gaze at it with
amazement.
They admit to
having not
seen such wonder
before either.
I am kind of
"King Cash" for a
few moments.

11:00 A.M. Monday, October 25 1948

My mother is at
Mrs. Clary's
classroom door.
Mrs. Clary sees her,
walks towards and
they talk.
Mother motions for
me to come outside,
stand before
her in a
dim hallway and
answer some questions.
My head is down and
I'm glad its dim
in that hallway.
She asks,
"Do you have any
spare money that
I can borrow?"
I hesitate,
thinking,
wondering if
I should come clean.
"I have a ten and a
twenty,"
I say,
knowing it is a
lie.
"Could I
borrow your money?"
"Sure,"
I answer.
We discuss reality,
talk about
knowing difference

between a ten and a
hundred dollar bill.
She never mentions
stealing.
I understand
everything, but
play dumb.

4:00 P.M. Monday, October 25 1948

My dad and
I quietly talk
after school.
He asks why
I took money from
his desk drawer.
I say,
"I need a little
pocket money."
I didn't admit to
showing off,
lying to Mother or that
I am a thief.

"Like an allowance?"
he questions.
"Yes."
We talk a bit about
earning an
allowance and
not taking money
without earning it.
"How about
fifty cents
per week?"
he asks.
We speak more

concerning truth and
honesty.
My father doesn't
moralize, but
points to pragmatic
behavior like
stealing and
being robbed,
cheating and
being cheated.
I understand a
great deal and
begin to recognize
true morality.
Morality seems
like a good
practical thing as
well as a good
church thing.

Riding Buses

I see Myrtle Turner
sitting behind a black
steering wheel of a
big yellow school bus,
waiting in front of
my house.
She is a big,
strong woman with
large arms and
legs.
I can see
her big right leg
angling towards
accelerator as
I climb two steps,
entering and
seeing only
two people.
Myrtle has an
impatient look on
her face, but
she is kind and
reasonable,
just not patient.
I think Myrtle
likes me and
thinks I'm cute.
I milk it a bit, but
not frequently.

I see brown
plastic covered
seats.

I pull myself
along an isle of
metal handles and
vinyl seats, and
finally swing into a
middle seat.
I get in trouble
occasionally on
Myrtle's bus and
sometimes have to
sit on a hot
bus heater
up front
beside her.

I hate that hot seat.
It is embarrassing, but
I cannot help but
misbehave
once in awhile.
I accept a
little misbehavior as a
fact of life.
I fear that
I shall misbehave
some forever and
suspect there will
always be a
hot heater to
sit on in my life,
one place or
another, but
I am determined to
sit there infrequently.

That heater is
like a painted line, a

sand line, a
rope line.
I plan to only
place a
misbehaving foot
over that line,
not step over it completely.
Sort of like
placing one butt cheek
on a prescribed
hot heater.
I think that
I will thus be
safe enough.
I think
my ass will not
get burned.
I think
my life will not
go up in flames.

Oregon Baptist Church

I feel
uncomfortable,
sitting in a
Sunday school class,
attempting to learn
about God.
My teacher asks
me to read aloud.
I cannot because of
Mrs. Clary's instilled
impediment.

There are just
too many hard words
in a thick Bible.
I am only
eight years old.
How can she expect
me to read
those words?
I try, but cannot.
She chooses
someone else, an
older kid, a
religious kid.
I think,
I will not return to
Sunday school class.

I can't feel
God here anyway.
Maybe I need to
go where hearing

God is taught or
where God teaches a
more natural way.
They say these are
His words, but
I can't read or
understand them.
I need simple
explanations to
complicated questions.

I yet feel
something other than
embarrassment
inside stirring,
something calming that
I cannot explain.
Something Mrs. Clary
can never take away.
It's something
bigger than
I can describe,
understand or
demonstrate.
I suspect only
God knows
what it is.

Railroad Tracks

In constant
images flickering,
I see my dad and
me walking near a
long earthen mound
abandoned years ago.
It looks similar to a
dyke or dam, but
there's no water present.
It's an old Inurban
right of way
located near modern
railroad tracks.
My dad says
it's from an
urban system of
trolleys that
ran parallel to
railroad tracks.
He says, "I used to
ride it from
Shelburn to
Terre Haute
when younger."

We silently look for
mushrooms,
finding few and
getting bored.
We suspect a
train coming and
put an ear to
steel shiny tracks,

feeling and hearing
faint vibrations.
We roadway lay near
steel tracks,
on our stomachs
about four feet away and
wait.
My dad says,
"Lay still,
don't stand up or the
rushing train air
might suck you under."
I lay perfectly still with
building anticipation,
heart pounding,
mind recording and
filming everything.
A train soon appears
out of eye corner,
moving towards with
powerful loudness.
I see it coming,
hear its rumble,
feel its vibration as
steel wheels nearer roll.
It's finally upon us,
streaking by,
vibrating my guts.
Tons and tons of
energy passes by
my teacup size eyes,
fixed straight ahead.
I want to close
my eyes, but
don't want to
miss a second of
fearful excitement.

It's a scary blur.
My mouth is dry,
speechless.
I'm scared to near death,
remaining quiet and
brave.
I don't stand,
even though,
wishing to do so.
I want to stand or at
least crawl and
then run away.
Without thought or
sense of courage,
I instinctively lay
with faith in my dad,
whose loving hand is
on my back.
I stick it out
until all is again
quiet and safe,
safe as an unfound
mushroom.

My Dad

My dad is
manly big,
six feet four,
two-hundred and
sixty pounds.
I see him at age
twenty-seven,
year I was born.
He's wearing a
white dress shirt,
black trousers and
shiny shoes.
He is holding
my sister Venita.

A would be
football lineman
he is, except
he slightly played,
quitting school at
sixteen.
He is often
amused by
subtle things,
seldom laughs, but
grins much.

He plays little at
anything,
works hard at
everything.
He loves to
work and
accomplish things.

His intelligence
carries
him through a
successful life where
he teaches
me more than
I can express.
In my nature
grows
honest and
true traits
given me to
last two lifetimes.

His big hands,
eighteen ring size,
are strong, but
gentle.
His voice
deep, but
soothing.
His belief in
God covert, but
apparent in
dealing with
all natural things.

He is
many things, but
truck driver and
farmer come to
mind first, but
second, a thinker,
inventor and
philosopher.

He is a man,
husband and
father.
He is
my full time hero,
compared to
my part-time hero
Duncan Reed.

o

I used to think that
I was but a child
forever lifted from
sheltered realm and
heaven sent gleam.

I then reasoned being a
drop flowing towards
fulfillment with other
rain drops gathering to
become a mighty force.

I was flowing water
cumulatively seeking
least resistance place, a
sparkling entity
heading homeward.

Roxie Hunt

I see my
old school where
Roxie Hunt is
our janitor and
Albert Laforge,
our maintenance man.
Roxie sweeps and
polishes floors while
Albert fixes things and
stokes steam boilers.
People respect them,
depend on them,
call them good friend.

Roxie always gives us
attention during recess and
lunchtime.
He sits and talks with us,
later cleans up after us.
His mind is dirt free,
manners correct and
life orderly.
He puts in
added hours after school,
making it clean and
shiny, and
pleasant smelling.
I can smell it now,
that small school of
two hundred and
fifty students in
K-12.

I nearly feel
boiler room
warmth from hot
fire boxes below
four huge boilers.
I see red hot coals
inside them as
Albert scoops in
more coal to
create steam for
two buildings.
There are two men
smoking cigarettes.
Several men
socialize here
during basketball
half time.
My dad is frequently
one of those smokers.
I consider smoking
someday also, but
not while playing
basketball.
My dad says,
"It would be like
wearing a log chain
around your neck."
When I get older,
I will be upstairs
in a small gymnasium
playing basketball,
having no interest in
boiler rooms.
I clearly future see that
small gym

crowded with people,
cheering and
encouraging me to
play basketball well.

6:00 P.M. Wednesday, January 12, 1949

For now, I rely on
imagination for
I have just begun to
play organized
basketball.
I have seen
few games in
what now seems a
large gymnasium.
There are bleacher seats
on one side and a
stage on other side.
Wooden benches are at
one end and a
padded wall on other.

Roxie Hunt
helps place chairs
everywhere possible as
people line up
for tickets.
It is universe center for
many people on a
Friday night during
cold winter.
Small town heroes are
made in hundreds of
small gymnasiums
throughout Indiana on
Friday nights.

I imagine myself
such a hero on
Friday nights at
Pimento High School.
I'm only
eight years old, but
I dream like a
sixteen year old.
Come spring,
state tournament
sectionals will
clearly separate
champion men from
ordinary boys of
which most players are
only pretenders.

How is it that
Roxie became a true
man to respect at
only five feet
seven inches and
never playing
basketball?
I am thinking
character counts a
lot these days.
My dad explains
character to me, but
I lack understanding.
I surely hope
I have it someday.

Chapter VI

MARCH 1949

Sunday	Monday	Tuesday	Wednesday	Thursday	Friday	Saturday
		1	2	3	4	5
6	7	8	9	10	11	12
13	14	15	16	17 St Patrick's Day	18	19
20	21	22	23	24	25	26
27	28	29	30	31		

www.freeprintablecalendar.com

Accepting Guilt

I'm not a
trick flyer,
wildcatter or
gambler.

I'm not a
Vegas kind of guy.
I'm no
Wayne Settles.

3:15 P.M. Saturday, March 7, 1949

Peanut

I caused my brother,
Warren, to suck a
peanut into his lung.
He was almost three and
I nearly eight years old.
I felt guilty, but
everyone honestly said
it wasn't my fault.

o

Warren and
I are back seat
laughing in our
black forty-nine
Plymouth sedan
sitting in front of
our house.
Warren begins
coughing.
He coughs for an
hour or so and
then quits.
No one is
concerned until
he starts
coughing again a
few days later.

3:15 P.M. Thursday, March 10, 1949

My parents
take him to a

local doctor, then to a
Terre Haute hospital.
They x-ray
his lungs and
find a peanut
in his lung.
It is causing
pneumonia and
of course has to
be removed.
They cut a slit in
his neck,
extracting it
with a special
clamping
instrument,
down through
trachea and
into lung.

I film his scar and
yet distinctly see it
in my mind.
I hear Mother say,
"We are lucky
it didn't fall apart
during removal."
I also film see her
holding Warren close,
long and frequently
after that incident.

3:15 P.M. Thursday, March 31, 1949

A couple weeks later,
we are laughing again,
but not while

eating peanuts.
I think I will always
carry that
memory film with me.
I see those
few minutes in a
special
mental movie.
I feel a
tinge of guilt and
humility; and
yet, many
mental movies
give me hope and
confidence,
spirituality and
faith.
That particular one
remains a learning,
grounding movie and
source for
brotherly love.

Highway Flares

Bill Compton and
my dad are
planting corn with
our new four row
corn planter.
I am playing in a
big white barn nearby.
My dad is renting
two farms west of
Pimento from
people who own
Willis Bottle Gas
in Terre Haute.
Bill is their
farm manager.

I find a highway flare
in a red metal box.
It looks like dynamite, but
directions say it's a flare.
I silently read instruction
pretty well for my age.
I strike it to action,
not knowing is purpose or
resulting potential.
It comes to life with
enormous white light and
sulfur smelling smoke.
I'm nearly trapped inside as
smoke fills barn and
my vulnerable lungs are
saying enough, enough.
I manage to escape

while coughing,
wheezing and
gasping for fresh air.
I manage to bring
my spectacular flare
out with me and
don't burn down
Bill's beautiful barn.
I feel lightheaded with
lungs burning horribly.
I can barely breath.
I'm lucky to be alive.

9:00 A.M. Wednesday, May 20, 1949

My lungs are
yet rattling and
wheezing a
week later, but
I cannot tell
my parents
what happened.
I am a bad,
foolish and
ignorant boy.
I learn
hard ways, but
my movies
easily recollect
lessons learned.
Innocence and
ignorance are
no excuse.
I wish experience
keeps me flare-less
in barns, but I fear
I am hopeless.

Hero

I see Duncan shooting
hook-shots with either hand,
wooing girls and leading with
strength and cool.
I see myself following
his example,
playing basketball,
shooting with either hand,
pursuing girls, leading with
strength and cool.

I see myself in a long line of
heroes at my little school.
I see myself walking shiny halls, using
Duncan as a template for success.

Today I am getting a
vaccination at school.
I'm sitting, waiting for a
needle to be put into
my arm, waiting unafraid for
Duncan gave me good advice.
"Relax," a nurse says, but
I will not relax for
Duncan told me,
"Flex your muscle as
tight as possible and
then it won't hurt."
"Relax," she says again.
"No," I retort,
"Duncan told me to
hold my arm tight."
"Ok, have it your way,"

she says with a head shake
while jamming a hug
hypodermic needle
in my rock hard arm.
It hurts like hell.
I'm thinking Duncan lies.

3:30 P.M. Tuesday, October 11, 1949

I am shooting
hook shots with
either hand and
leading with strength and
cool, but I don't
see myself being like
Duncan in many ways.
I am losing my hero.
His image is fading as
I learn more about him.
He's not such a good guy.
He's a fighter, a
brother shotgun shooter and
who knows what else.
He's not what I thought.
He's not like my first hero,
my dad, who never
shot a hook-shot in
his life, but knows how to
play life's game fairly.
He never lies or
gives me bad advice.
I have only one hero.

Half Man

I am driving
tractors and
pickup trucks,
helping till
fields with
Father by
my side at
nine years old.

He lets me steer,
pull plow rope and
line-up furrows,
allowing
me to gauge
corners and
define
straight lines.

I'm a good
driver,
it's as if
I can drive
anything and
it helps that
I'm big for
my age.

Our hired hand
quit today,
getting enough
bicycle buying money.
My dad asks if
I want to work,

helping plow with a
small tractor.

He says,
"If you get tired and
want to play or
take a nap,
just stop."
So I get on our
Farmall H and
begin plowing.

I plow and plow,
never quit, and
think little about
play or naps as if
half a man
struggling to be
all man like
my dad.

Glass Full of Cherries

My sister Venita
practices a 4-H
demonstration on
how to make a
cherry pie.
My mother buys
pre-sweetened
cherries
five gallons
at a time.

I love Venita's
pies, but
also sneak and
eat frozen cherries.
I scoop them
into a glass and
eat like ice cream.
They are dwindling.

Mother buys more
unsweetened cherries.
She speaks only
once about
declining cherries.
"It's almost as if
someone else is
baking pies
besides Venita,"
she sarcastically says.

I'm not eating
frozen unsweetened

cherries,
not because
they are bitter, but
because my mother is
letting me off
without penalty.
She's teaching with
innuendo and charm.

My parents'
self-discipline
teaching methods
begin subtly.
Stricter ways are
always available.
Subtly is usually
effective
when a little boy
has a conscience.

Uncle Wayne

My Uncle Wayne is
taking me up in
his airplane today.
It's a sunny day,
no wind, no clouds.
It's my first time
flying and
I'm excited.

Uncle Wayne is a
gambler in
many ways,
going to Las Vegas
four times a year.
He's been a
millionaire twice and
lost most of it twice.
He's working on
his third million,
wildcatting for oil.
He knows how to
make money, but
not how to keep it.

We fly northward
from Sullivan.
I see far horizon in
misty haze,
remaining fixed while
powerful engine
hums and
pushes us forward.
I hear wind

slipping past
my window without
flying sensation.
It's not what
I imagined.
It seems like
we're sitting still in
mid morning air at
three thousand feet.

Uncle Wayne asks,
"How you like it?"
I say, "Ok, but
it's a little boring."
"You want me to
do some tricks,
make it more exciting?"
"Sure," I answer.

Uncle Wayne
flew airplanes in
Korea and was a
Navy test pilot
during its end.
He tested a
new type of airplane
called a jet.
Uncle Wayne knows
dog fighting.
He knows air tricks.

In minutes,
I'm sick and
throwing-up on
Uncle Wayne's
beautiful split-tail
Beachcraft Bonanza

airplane.
We land.
I apologize while
angry at myself,
embarrassed and
humiliated.
I thank him,
believing
he'll never
take me up again.
I'm not a
trick flyer,
wildcatter or
gambler.
I'm not a
Vegas kind of guy.
I'm no
Wayne Settles.

Broken Plans

I see a fence post pile
while riding Patsy,
my now favorite pony.
I prod her to jump.
She wishes to resist, but
relents to my command.
Over we flow as if one,
boy and pony in
joyful triumph.
Again, we trace an arc from
one side to other,
jumping through air with
little resistance.
I sense Patsy
wishing to rebel as
we gallop a sweeping circle,
heading towards woodpile.
I release rein tension as
we approach,
pressing my heels into
her soft sides and
lifting with anticipation.
Patsy at last moment
darts to my right,
not jumping, but
skirting around post pile
while I fly over it,
landing with arms extended.
Hands push earth and
arms bend, accepting
body weight.
I lie a few moments in
confusion as Patsy runs

towards a pasture gate.
My arm hurts,
probably broken.
I've had enough
jumping for one day.

6:30 P.M. Wednesday, June 28, 1950

I'm home from
Sullivan Hospital where
I got my arm set and
put in a cast for
eight long weeks.
"How will I eat?"
I asked my dad.
"With your left hand,"
he explains.
"Oh, and write and
shoot baskets?"
He says, "Everything."
I start my new
left hand living
immediately at lunch,
then practice writing.
I then shoot
some baskets.
My world is back
in order.
My broken plans are
mending.
I just can't
summer swim
for a while at
Shakamak State Park.

I practice set and
hook shots as
summer progresses,
arm mends and
time passes quickly.
I learn that
plans change and
life transforms.
Things break and
things mend.
I'm not, however,
too young to
understand that
some things
will not mend.
I am afraid life is
more complicated
than a broken arm.
Transformation,
alteration and
amendment seeks
my mind, and
I soul record it all as
movies in my head.

Grand Champion Steer

I clearly see
my big red
Grand Champion
shorthorn steer.
He trails behind as
I lead him at
Vigo County's
fairgrounds.
He is huge,
weighing over
eleven-hundred
pounds.
His beautiful
black eyes and
black nose shine in
mid-day sun.
His sweaty coat
glistens from hot
August day heat.

I walk near
his head,
avoiding
large hooves that
once crushed
my foot.
He has no idea
his size and has
no avoiding foot
manners.
He is only a
year old, but is
massive from

eating nutritiously.
He is a pet,
friend and
4-H project.
Thing is,
I will later
sell him at
auction, and
I know
I will cry.
I am eleven
years old and can
yet secretly cry.

I am big for eleven, but
must remember that
he is an eleven
hundred pound
steer with mindless
overwhelming strength.
I lead him towards a
grandstand where
auctioneers are about to
solicit bids.
It is a tranquil walk with
yielding clay racetrack
beneath feet and
soft grandstand light
beckoning me and
my steer to come closer.

An amplified voice
suddenly bellows and
echoes through
grandstand air.
My champion
goes crazy.

We are first in line and
he has no time to
get accustomed to an
amplified, blaring
auctioneer voice.
My big friend's
black eyes
roll white and
his black mouth
turns red while
wailing a sound
I have never heard.

He darts,
racetrack runs and
I cannot hold
him back or
run alongside.
He pulls me,
feet digging into
soft clay.
I finally lose
my footing.
He drags me,
feet yet digging into
soft orange clay,
hands yet gripping
lead rein.
I will not let go.
He is racetrack
dragging me with
more than
five hundred people
watching.
He finally stops,
too fat to run and
too scared to

decide where to escape.
I finally with help
maneuver him in a
small circle while
auctioneer chants and
buyers bid on
my beautiful friend's
fate.

Sadly I know
it is all part of
growing up on a
reality teaching farm.
Knowing truth and
abiding actuality is
part of maturity
in general, but
emotionally difficult.
Fantasy often
flits through
my innocent mind, but
reality now overwhelms.
Growing up on a
farm teaches that
animals come and go.
I, however, yet
remember his name,
"Big Red," and
someone saying,
"You shouldn't
name him, just
give him a number,
don't get too attached."
I didn't listen.

Lesson Learned

I stand near gasoline pump,
near circular stone driveway.
Mother reprimands me for
making brother, Warren, cry.

I disrespectfully talk back.
I am cocky, full of myself.
I am big, Mother is small,
I feel manly at twelve.

She threatens to spank me,
then decides switching is better.
She has threatened this before,
but never followed through.

She usually disciplines subtly.
I challenge, but she insists.
I say, "I'm too big to spank."
She nearby Maple tree points.

"I'm too big to switch."
We argue, she gets frustrated.
She picks up rocks, throws them,
yells curse words while crying.

She never curses, forbids it.
I remain manly, a soldier, a
tough guy until she retreats.
I then feel sorrowful.

I am ashamed, feel guilty,
but don't follow to apologize.
Warren silently watches,
wondering if he is next.

My dad wishes to speak
concerning my mother
when he comes home.
"You're too big to spank?"

He pauses, then softly asks,
"Big enough for an ass kicking?"
His conviction permeates.
I feel dominated, humiliated.

I now know Mother's feelings.
"Maybe not." I humbly say.
We talk about respect, mother,
all people, and I understand.

I humbly shake his huge hand
with empathy for humanity.
I apologize to sweet Mother,
step closer to true manhood.

I self vow to never dominate,
humiliate or threaten others,
choose switching over making
someone cry, no matter what.

Naydean

My dad and
I drive by
Joe Moore's farm with
big barns and a
beautiful house.
I think Joe is
rich, and from what
my dad says,
he takes in kids
who have no
parents or are
troubled.
That's all
I know about kids
who get on and
off my
school bus there
every day and
change nearly
every year.
They come and go.
Some stay a
short while,
some a few years.
Naydean is one of
those kids.

Joe raises,
trains and events
show horses for
other people.
I don't know
anything about

his horses, except
they are expensive and
special.
I see them
while passing by
his farm.

I am interested in
his horses, but
don't know Joe.
I'm more interested in
Naydean Oliver and
down deep inside
want to know
her better.

7:15 A.M. Monday, October 13, 1952

My school bus
stops at Joe's house
on highway 246,
picking up Naydean.
She steps up into
Myrtle's bus,
turns and walks
slowly past me.
I can smell
fresh morning
soap fragrance from
her passing breeze.
Her long wavy
red hair dances about
her face.
I can't help but
notice her
full red lips as
she smiles at me.

She is wearing a
thin flowered
dress that
reveals her curvy
body parts.

Naydean is sixteen.
I am twelve, but
I can't keep
my sheepish eyes
off her totality.
She scares me, yet
I am intrigued.

She sits in a
seat directly
behind me and
taps my shoulder.
"I could just
kiss you,
you sweet
little boy,"
she says to me.
Oh, I am
embarrassed.
I wonder if anyone
heard her.
"Let me give you
one little kiss,"
she resumes.
She grabs
my shoulder and
tries to spin
me around.
I jump over
two seats to escape.
She aisle follows.

Myrtle yells,
"Phillip sit down.
No, better yet,
come up here,
sit behind me."
She rearview mirror
looks again.
"Naydean,
sit and behave."

I do as told.
Naydean squirms in
her seat.
I have been in this
seat before.
I try to behave, but
it's not easy.
I have a feeling
Naydean will never
really sit down and
behave in life.
I don't put
much faith in
me behaving
either, I guess.

I know there will
come a time when
I wish Naydean
would kiss me.
In fact,
kiss me on
my forehead,
cheeks and
lips when
we're alone.

I don't mind being
embarrassed, but
not in front of
other kids.
She looks like
one of those
models in a
Paul Chris
barbershop magazine.
I hope she doesn't
forget to tease me
another day.
Maybe next time,
I won't run away.

7:15 A.M. Monday, December 15, 1952

Naydean
never bothers
me anymore,
only smiles once
in awhile.
She knows I think
she is beautiful.

She doesn't get on
my bus today.
Myrtle says
she moved, but
Joe didn't move.
Maybe she wishes
not to stay at
Joe's anymore.
Little does she know
I would help her
if I could.
I miss Naydean.

Life Is a Mystery

I can nearly see
inside my body,
watching electricity
flit through brain,
red blood flow
through veins and
muscles flexing.
I can nearly see
my heart beating,
lungs expanding and
eyes seeing.

I question.
How can an eye
see itself?
Through pre-recorded
mental movies
seen in retrospect,
I answer.

Oh, wonder of it all,
mystery of life,
all astounds me
to no end.
Do not try
telling me that
everything happens
by accident.
Body processes are
divine guided
evolution and
secretly planned.
I can nearly see

inside my mind,
soul and
spirit, and yet,
cannot find them.
They too are
divinely created and
secretly planned,
hidden also in
wondrous awe.

And from where comes
this knowledge?
I ask while reading
National
Geographic and
listening to
Oliver Reed
speak about religion.
I look inside and
see movies of
my vivid past.
I look towards
heaven for
my muted future.
An inner voice
speaks and I listen.

About this suspicious
knowledge,
I cannot talk of
with others, for
it seems insane or
just stupid.

My Song

I recall and
hear a melody.
My essence is
beginning to
film with a
yesterday living
theme song.
A thousand
moments grasp
time,
standing still, then
moving and melding
together like an
inevitable grinding
glacier.
My world is
becoming shared
moments to
remember.
I sing and
relinquish nothing.
Everything is a
new living film.
I sway to an
essence melody.
I dance to intense
heart beat.
I am alive.

7:15 A.M. Monday, January 5, 1953

Pitts Family

On a cold January day,
just after Christmas,
my bus stops at a gray
weather-beaten house where
twenty-one thin children embark.
They are his, hers and
ours Pitts children.
I can only guess what
Christmas was like for them.
I see little joy on their faces,
little enthusiasm in their voices,
little fight in their souls.
I film-reflect my blessings.
I feel guilty for all that I possess.
Last bus stop was Piety's
who are Florida winter staying.
I yet, however, cannot judge
love and joy in others.
I cannot judge blessings
in disguise.
I yet see poverty as
never a good friend.
I see little as not a good thing.
Pitts children as strangers to me,
I feel ashamed.

o

The Pitts family lived in
my township only a half year,
our trustee said, "no more free stuff,
no more handouts," for he had
little to share and no more to give.

Chapter VII

JANUARY 1954

Sunday	Monday	Tuesday	Wednesday	Thursday	Friday	Saturday
					1 New Year's Day	2
3	4	5	6	7	8	9
10	11	12	13	14	15	16
17	18	19	20	21	22	23
24	25	26	27	28	29	30
31						

Finding Self

I see a large
Indiana Theater stage and a
movie screen as

I play own mind
movie while watching
Charlton Heston in
"The Ten
Commandments."

Life is Simple

One simple life aim is finding,
"Thyself," in a complex world,

another is teaching that
most are hopefully happy,

another is searching for one
significant self attribute,

another is writing a yarn based on
one's amazing experience,

another is gaining wisdom
enough for heaven's big book,

and last is being spiritual
enough to fruitfully impress God.

o

I began thinking
too much at an
early age, but
soon learned that
thinking too much is
better than
thinking too little.

Straightening Teeth

I sucked my thumb
when younger.
My mother tried to
bad habit break me.
I'm not sure when
I quit, but still
wound up with
buckteeth.

o

I had buckteeth,
surely didn't
like them, but
my parents couldn't
afford braces.
No one around
my neighborhood
got them anyway.

I considered
how braces
work and
decided that
I could put
pressure
on my teeth
just like braces.

o

I mind film see
myself constantly

pressing against
two front teeth,
sitting around
doing nothing and
driving a tractor
doing little.

I look
in a mirror,
seeing my teeth
nearly straight and
say, superb mind,
you help
me constantly
in time of need.

I'm finding that
I possess
inductive and
deductive reasoning.
I'm only fourteen,
yet see myself as a
thinker and a
problem solver.

I spend much time
thinking and
pressing teeth while
on a tractor
plowing, disking,
planting and
cultivating crops with
my dad.

He's a thinker, a
philosopher and an
achiever.

I have a good life,
pressing teeth,
pressing mind,
playing movies of
me pressing life.

I'm constantly
remembering
what was and
dreaming about
what might be, and
filming everything
in my head for
future watching.

o

I straightened crooked teeth
without expensive braces.
Straightening mind wasn't as easy.
I, however, have a great smile and a life
without undue pressure or stress.

James Dean

My projector is clicking and
hot mental light is glowing.
I'm outside Terre Haute's
long ago constructed Indiana Theater.

o

I pass through
heavy brass doors and
enter a thirty-foot
high domed lobby,
decorated with
ornate ceiling
sculptures and
mutely painted
nature scenes.
I silently pass through
another doorway
into a huge dimly
lit lobby and
then into a
theater where
"Rebel
Without a Cause,"
is playing.

I have no idea who
James Dean is, but am
soon to find out.
I hear someone
whisper that
he's a Hoosier from
Fairmont, Indiana.

I watch James Dean
come to life in
Hollywood fashion.
I play own scenes in
my expanding mind,
making my own movie,
putting myself in
his character part.
James continually
inspires me to also be
rebellious.
I can't remember
his movie
character name.
I only remember
James Dean.
I want to be
James Dean.
I want to be
rebellious, but
I'm not
quite sure how to
go about it.
I want a black
forty-nine Mercury.

10:15 P.M. Saturday, March 6, 1955

My adjusting eyes
see familiar soundings:
brass doors,
marquee, and
seventh and Ohio
streets as
I theater exit.
It's dark now,
people, mostly

young people, are
milling around.
I'm with a group
waiting for
our ride home.

Two tall guys from
Gerstmyer Tech
approach me.
They're basketball players.
One of them is
Howard Dardeen.
He's six feet four and a
mature senior.
I'm six feet one and
only a freshman.
I saw him play at
Evansville,
semi-finals last year.
I wonder why
he's looking at me.
I'm nobody.
"How's the movie?"
he asks.
I go into a long
movie description, and
of course, describe
James Dean.
"So you liked it?"
he continues to question.
"You play basketball?"
"Sure, all the time."
I answer quickly.
"I thought so.
Ok, see you."

They both nod and

towards theater walk.
I think they have
me confused with
someone else or
maybe think I'm
Terry Dishinger.
We sort of look alike,
except Terry Dishinger is
six feet seven.
He plays basketball at
Garfield.

I feel great, discovering
James Dean and
having two big city
high school
basketball players
talk to me.
I think I'm cool,
cool as James Dean.

o

I heard from a friend that
Howard Dardeen lives in
Indianapolis and is yet
playing basketball at
age fifty-two.
I had two more
experiences with him, but
won't talk about it now.

Hypnotizing

I hypnotize myself,
lying face up on
my bed while one
spot on ceiling staring.
I stare until myopic,
becoming visually and
mentally blank.
That spot is now
universe center.
I then recall created
movies in my head.
I have done this
many times before.
It seems natural and
easy as time passes with
decreasing intensity.

I regress into
personal history archives,
playing movies from a day,
week, month ago.
I condense and simplify,
watching while quickly
regressing until being a
small child, toddler, baby.
I revert farther and
farther until finding myself
in my mother's womb, in
pre-birth time, in heaven.
I am transitional material,
becoming less until a
baby, fetus, zygote.

9:30 P.M. Thursday, April 14, 1955

I am in trouble.
I can't consciously
return to my ceiling,
bed, room.
I can't find way back.
I am near panic scared,
in darkness stuck.
Finally, calmness and
thinking return me.
Present time environs
become clearer as
I slowly movie watch
my way home.

9:00 A.M. Friday, April 15, 1955

I decide to quit
hypnotizing myself,
being afraid of
not next time
returning to my bed,
room, reality.
I instead real time
movie watch
in conscious awareness,
seeking knowledge and
wisdom retrospection.

Manly Plans

I wish to enter, to
see important
girl stuff within
Venita's room.
I look inside,
intrigued as if
it is a magical place,
packed with secrets.
Blinds and curtains are
pulled, creating soft and
comfortable light.
Intrigue haunts.

o

I am interested in
her friends, like
Ruth Ann Hicks.
Maturity is flirting with
my private parts.
Mind movies are
creatively changing
boyish ideas into
manly plans,
present reality into
future dreams.
Fantasy intrigues.

Plans

I think about
Soon being out
On my own,
Checking things out
Away from home.
I don't need a
Mother or
Father.
I don't need a
Mrs. Moore in
My life.
I need a
Sweet young
Miss Moore.
I am nearly a
Man with
Manly ideas and
Plans.
I am expanding
My territory.
I am becoming
Worldly.
I am fifteen and
Anything is possible.
I need to fly.
I need to soar
Like an eagle.

o

Dreams, schemes and hormones
caused a boy's mind and body to warily
glean, scatter and sow stupidity.

DC Case

It is fifty-two degrees,
morning dew is
nearly burned off as
warm sunlight bakes
my already
suntanned skin.
My dad and I are
plowing a front
forty-acre field with
two DC Case tractors,
pulling fourteen inch
three bottom plows.
We intend finishing by
eight hours away dusk.

Our DC Case
tractors are like
big orange monsters
turning over soil with
straight pipes belching
roaring exhaust.
I think we are
big time farmers,
believing that people
judge a farmer by
tractor size and
number owned.
We have two
big ones and
two small ones.
Attached implements
seem nearly immaterial
compared to tractor size.

We both have
attached umbrellas to
protect our skin from
day's long hot
summer sun.
I am dark completed,
getting that from
my mother, but
my dad is pure
German white.
He has typical
farmer tan areas, like
lower face and arms.
He reveals
few body parts.
His legs are so white
they reflect sunlight and
hurt my eyes.
I am deep brown, but
I can yet burn and
don't want to
get darker.
I have contrasting
blue eyes,
seventy-five percent
German, but
who would know it with
my dark skin.

A girl with
my coloring
once called me a
German gypsy and
asked,
"Do you know
how many gypsies

Hitler killed?"
"I don't know,"
I replied.
I later found an
answer,
many thousands.
I think about that
now as I plow.
I think about
Hitler frequently.
Germany is
my fatherland.
WW II is not that
long ago.
I wonder about
possible family in
Germany.

My mind wanders,
nearly blank,
reality unaware,
fostering imagination.
I think of a
thousand things,
plowing takes
little concentration.

I play a hundred
movies in
my head while
driving my DC Case
tractor; as
it monotonously
crawls up and down a
forty acre field
this May day.
I am sixteen.

My father is forty-four.
I wonder how many
movies will
I have created by
my father's age.
Our DC Case tractors
will be antiques by then.
I wonder who
will help him
plow this field then.
Surely not me for
I'll be gone
seeking an
expanding world that
seeks my attention.

o

Expanding time
brings baffling wind,
seeking answers of a
howling mind.

Hope answers not,
like disturbing
dreams dreamt or
ruthless wind spent.

A frail naive tree,
stands against
wind and can't
pray for survival.

Understanding,
like mysterious wind,
eludes wary eyes
wishing to perceive.

First Car

I picture
my first car, then
start my mind
projector and
walk around it,
look inside,
capture its beauty
on my birthday.

o

It's a black
fifty-four Ford with
plenty of chrome.
It's shiny and
polished clean.

I raise its hood,
seeing a flathead
V-8 engine.
Car dealer,
Benny Easter,
says a little old lady
owned it and
I believe him.
It is in perfect
condition, being
three years old.

My dad
bought it

151

just before my
sixteenth birthday,
now giving
it to me on
my birthday.
I have to work
two summers to
pay for it.
He is more than
generous,
counting two
working summers,
five-hundred dollars
each summer.

Of course,
I have already
worked hard
five summers and
will work many
more summers, but
we both are
happy.

3:00 P.M. Sunday, June 9, 1957

I drive to
Carolyn Lloyd's
house during
my first time
out by myself.

I like Carolyn,
she is pretty and
lives close.
I wish to
impress her.

I take her for a
short ride.
She seems
unimpressed.
I think
I'll probably
not go back.

9:00 A.M. Monday, August 5, 1957

I next see
my first love,
Jackie.
She is impressed with
my car and
I'm impressed with
her.

We
ride around with
her blond hair
flying from
downed windows.
I see myself in a small
rearview mirror with a
Cheshire cat smile.

9:00 A.M. Monday, August 12, 1957

Oh, melancholy joy
you soothe
my soul for
I can feel a
fifty-four Ford
steering wheel in hands,
hear exhaust in ears,
see dust flying with

eyes and notice
my "awe of life"
expression
in rearview mirror.

Projector clicking
sound fades and
light goes dim.
Moving pictures
slow and then
only a picture of
my black Ford
remains with
Jackie and me
standing beside
it in front of
my red brick
high school building.

1:00 P.M. Sunday, August 18, 1957

I drive my car on a narrow Indiana gravel road,
dust and stones cause tires to wander and slide.
I slow and stop near a fast moving creek.

There is a flat concrete slab near creek's bank
jutting out, fighting to remain fixed to a steep bank.
I turn key, park car and walk to water's edge.

I imagine, from concrete remains, a once small
grist mill grinding fresh wheat into flour with a
large round stone turned by a wooden water wheel.

It is a bright sunny day, full of hope as a sojourn
begins that will last a lifetime, for this day in August,
I realize machine and mind mobility, and true freedom.

Ten Commandments

I see a large
Indiana Theater stage and a
movie screen as
I play own mind
movie while watching
Charlton Heston in
"The Ten
Commandments."
My date is from
Patoka, Indiana.
I met her yesterday.
She is visiting
John D. Turner and
his family for a
few summer days.
I probably ask her out
just to show-off
my car, mobility and
big city life.

I am taking a chance
on a religious movie,
knowing little about
Bible commandments.
I remember some
from visiting
Oregon Baptist Church a
few times.
I'm not religious,
however, that is
changing while
watching Moses with
his stick,

his two slates and
his God
driven influence.
I hide
my tears during
more than one
movie scene.
Someone or
something is
affecting
my sense of self.
I'm embarrassed.
I suspect that
I'm becoming a
little spiritual
tonight without
reasoning, but with
subconscious
divine awareness.

10:30 P.M. Saturday, October 5, 1957

I'm alone in my room,
two hours after
my spiritual experience.
I see myself yet in that
balcony, row and seat.
I suspect that
I will figuratively
sit in that seat
throughout my life and
replay that
Moses movie
over and over again
in my head.
I suspect that
I will replay

my own
Moses movies
over and over again
in my head.

I am still
seeing and
feeling,
breathing and
weeping,
absorbing and
relenting own
Moses effect.
I know not what is
happening to me,
sitting here alone, but
surely not alone.
I am different from a
few hours ago.
I am losing
innocence and
gaining wisdom, and
cannot tell
anyone about
my newly found
spiritualism.
I'm not sure, but
I suspect that
I have soul,
whatever that is.
I feel a little
Moses within
me tonight.

11:30 A.M. Friday, October 11, 1957

Peely Paul

I went to
my fifty-year
high school reunion and
found nearly
everyone from
my class there,
except for,
"Peely" Paul Snyder,
who suddenly died a
couple of years ago.
It caused
my mental
movie mind to play
Peely Paul movies.

o

I film see
his pockmarked face with
red pimples dotting.
His nickname is
from burning
rubber off
his pickup
truck tires while
leaving school at
lunchtime.
I see him clearly in
his old black truck,
giving it gas while
sharply turning from
rock school driveway
onto asphalt street with

skillful precision.
He turns left quickly,
shifting weight right.
His left rear tire spins,
making a squeaking
sound as
blue smoke rolls.
We call it peeling tires.
I guess that Peely Paul
doesn't have a
promising future.
I watch him
peeling tires and
simultaneously smoking a
cigarette while
leaving school.

He's always on
his way to
Haley Beck's little
eight seat restaurant,
where there's hardly
enough room to
maneuver.
How she earns a
living in that
tiny place is a
mystery to me.
Peely and
Bill Bartlett
hang out there
every day.
Bill is kind of a
hoodlum,
our only one.
He stole some
diesel fuel from

Mr. Turner's
farm tank and
put it in
his car,
problem is,
he doesn't have a
diesel engine.
His exhaust is
smoking so much that
he can't escape
getting caught.
At least,
Peely's truck
isn't smoking.
I believe Peely is
truly honest.

My Friend Jim

Jim is slightly built,
five feet nine and
weighs one hundred and
thirty pounds.
He has a
narrow face,
wide nose and
full lips.
He is dark
completed, with
lighter skin beneath
his gold ring.
We are both
well suntanned.

We are best friends for
sure this summer.
I know his cousin
who has a
nice car like mine.
Jim and I cruise
everywhere while
talking cars, girls and
music.
We love
"Blues" music and
hang out at a
little restaurant
south of town with
blues music on an
old jukebox.
It's an odd place to
find blues.

I wish I knew that
restaurant's history.
I don't even know
who owns it.

We love blues and
sometimes listen to a
radio station in
Gallatin, Tennessee that
plays blues.
We can barely hear
it sometimes
because of static and
wavering signal.
A disk jockey
named "Big John R,"
keeps us entertained,
playing and
talking about blues, and
advertising
"White Rose Petroleum Jelly."
We don't know
what it is, but that
doesn't matter.
We imitate Big John R,
speaking southern
down home talk,
speaking black man
blues talk.

I gain an
education concerning
blues and
black man talk.
I occasionally
impersonate
Big John R.

Jim says I sound
just like him.
Jim says one time
he couldn't get on a
bus in Tennessee.
They said
he was too dark.
I don't understand.
I don't know
what it mattered.
I'll miss Jim.
He's going home at
summer's end.

o

I realized,
forty years later,
while thinking
about Jim, that
he was half-black.
Strange how
I was colorblind to
my friend Jim and
not blues music.

Duke

When I hear a
name like "Duke"
one person comes to
mind and creates,
revealing teen movies.
He represents
rock and roll fun in
Terre Haute that is
pure liberation.

I record times,
places and people.
I create films of
youth centers,
gymnasiums and
expressing kids
discarding
innocence of
mind and body.

I have a hundred
movies swirling in
my awesome head,
provoking life at
vulnerable seventeen,
defining mobile
freedom.

10:15 P.M. Saturday, July 12, 1958

I see rows of
metal chairs,
teenagers temporarily

sitting in them
while watching
loud rock-and-roll
bands and
groups perform.
I see a wide stage at
Schulte High School.
A nine-piece band is
playing favorite songs.

I then see a group,
"The Fascinators,"
coming on stage.
It's Jim Calvin's
eight man troop,
singing, dancing,
entertaining and
making an already
rowdy crowd
more rowdy.

Girls are screaming.
Guys are moving to
loud music beat.
Jim Calvin is a
smooth operator with a
slick tongue.
Everyone knows him as
"Duke."
His group's
choreography is
polished and
unique.
I have to admit,
his group is
quite fascinating.

Jim Calvin,
aka Duke, is cool.
Many girls wish to be
his woman,
hanging around
back stage as if
he's a rock star.
Ok, he is a
local rock star.

I know Jim from
Farmersburg.
His dad runs a
local barbershop.
He's no different
from me, except
he has arrogance,
attitude and
confidence.
I don't have those
cool attributes.
He is on stage
moving like a
mad man,
singing heart out,
wooing girls.

I wonder what
he will be
when not
fascinating.
I wonder what
I will be
when not so shy,
reserved and
modest.

I have small picture
confidence.
It's big picture
confidence in which
I see self limitations.
I want to see
high standards,
big pictures,
big movies.
I yet think that
I can do anything.
I have inner
confidence and
outer skepticism.
I just need
exposure.
I imagine a vast
world out there,
far beyond a
limiting highway
between Pimento and
Terre Haute.

o

My twelve highway miles
soon became sixty,
then a hundred,
then six hundred and
then three thousand.
They finally became
five thousand skyway miles.
Time and distance became
freedom tools and
I recorded it all in my head.

Mort McCauley

Mort drives a shiny forty-two Ford hot rod.
He pulls next to me, heading in opposite direction.

My engine is silent while his is high-lift racing cam loping.
He is a tough looking, muscular Tech High School senior.

He has built and customized his car all by himself.
His huge upper arm is flat against a window doorframe.

His arm looks even larger, making him quite intimidating.
"Hey, you bastard, you never came to get those fenders."

I remain still, staring into his eyes with nothing to say.
"How come you never showed?" he says, pissed off.

"I think you got me mixed up with someone else."
"Oh, I'm sorry," he says and smiles. "Sorry, Man."

I know Mort from reputation and believe he is tough.
He started weight lifting railroad track in sixth grade.

He frequently trades for longer pieces at a local junk yard.
He now bench-presses about four-hundred fifty pounds.

I want Mort to be a friend of mine, but hold my ground.
I remain quiet, staring at him, pretending to be tough.

I finally return his smile and ask about his cool car.
We talk for awhile and both know we will be friends.

Mort hears carburetors sucking, engine loping and lifters
chattering when I start my engine, he grins and nods.

Film Making Tool

Car crazy guys cruise by
on Wabash Avenue,
passing near where
I'm parked at
my favorite
drive-in restaurant.
I have cruised
Wabash Avenue twice
myself tonight from
third to thirtieth street.

I like to hang-out,
pretending to be
James Dean.
I like being social,
pretending to be
extroverted, but
deep down inside
I'm introverted.

I love humanity, but
love few people.
I like to film them,
recording life in
own sociable way.
My car is a mobile
filmmaking tool and
my mind is
its limitless director.

Willows

Bending willows
switch and beat
my reminding soul,
allowing wind to
caress emotions softly.

I stand beneath
wind whipped limbs,
causing stinging flesh to
rebel and cry for
tomorrow's redemption.

Modest green
hanging limbs,
seemingly frail,
beat earth and me,
both willing to die.

Our roots seek depth
into earth's dark loam,
willow and me
seek grace,
learning to be holy.

We delicately earth
fall as organic refuge,
gently punished while
modestly waiting greater
self awareness.

Chapter VIII

AUGUST 1958

Sunday	Monday	Tuesday	Wednesday	Thursday	Friday	Saturday
					1	2
3	4	5	6	7	8	9
10	11	12	13	14	15	16
17	18	19	20	21	22	23
24	25	26	27	28	29	30
31						

www.PocketCalendar.com

Learning
Lessons

I meticulously prepare for
battle, where
I meditate before
knowing meditation, where
I psych myself before
knowing psychology,

where
I play mental movies of
past performances and
future successes.

Mind In Hand

I see myself
boyish chancing with
hands and mind.
It's like crushing rocks
causing blood to seep.
It's like following a
silver mind screen
towards tomorrow.

My mind
temporarily grasps
more than ordinary and
less than magnificent.
I record shapes
between radiant
film glow and
blackish night rebellion.

My mind guides while
living in retrospect,
knowing life after fact,
watching film too late.
All I can do is
desperately edit
when time allows and
desire demands.

o

My mind used to wander, meander, and roam to
unknown places, forms and intensities.
It now seeks its way like a river, a Zen river.

First Love

I see my
first love
in mind and
feel her
in heart.
We passionately
kiss and
fondle, but
never go
farther.

I am stupid
after a year or
so and push her
out of my life,
into another's
arms,
presuming to be a
macho man at
seventeen.

I, however,
must discover,
investigate and
experiment.
I am a result of
modern times and
mobility need.
I lose Jackie to a
man with a
white Corvette and
now I'm alone
in my black Ford.

o

An odd world
opens to me.
A world that
expands past
Mrs. Moore,
Ruth Ann and
Jackie.
I grow past
mother's
caress and
gentle nature,
past father's
stern advice and
patience.

I grow in an
intriguing world
beyond
Venita's room,
family farm,
shiny car and
imagination.
It is as if a
world conspiracy
has me by
neck's nape and
bent on innocence
destruction, and
I assert no known
resistance.

Driving Trucks

I drove anything with rubber tires and a
steering wheel at seventeen years old.

o

I see my dad's new red Dodge truck
in front of me on U.S. Highway 40.
I am following at a safe distance
in an older red Dodge straight truck.

We're hauling limestone from
Marshall, Illinois to a farm
south of Terre Haute, Indiana.
Farmers hire us to deliver and
spread limestone on their
acidic fields, causing soil to
become more alkaline.
Farmers pay for hauling while
government pays for limestone.

My dad hauls limestone and
makes good off-season money.
He loves trucks and loves to
drive trucks when not farming.
I gladly help him frequently
when not attending school.

Right now, we're traveling a
narrow two-lane highway.
We gain speed going downhill,
getting to sixty-five mph and
then slowly crawl to forty mph
up other side to hill's peak.

It's a bit scary shooting down a hill,
bouncing in seat while holding
tightly to a steering wheel with
eight tons of stone at my back.
I call it "rockin and rollin."
My dad calls it "real truckin."

We stop for weighing at an
Illinois boarder weigh station.
We're then heading for Terre Haute,
but now on flat Indiana concrete.
We will make five loads today.
My dad gets four dollars a ton,
four times eight tons, five trips
times two of us equals
three hundred twenty dollars.
Now that's good money in
nineteen-fifty-eight.
My dad often reminds me that
he has many expenses.
I listen and learn at our kitchen table
while my parents talk business.
It's hard, dusty work and a
little dangerous, but I don't
identify with danger at seventeen.
It's all fun to me.

o

*My dad had "Dale Reisner and Sons," painted on the doors of all
his trucks. He usually bought red single axle Dodge trucks. His last
truck, however, was a red tandem axle International that hauled
twelve instead of eight tons. It was his last limestone hauling truck.
He sold it and went out of business just before the government
stopped paying farmers for limestone. It was a smart move.*

Mike Carpenter

I mental movie see
Mr. Carpenter
standing at a
seventh and
Wabash
street corner,
waving hello and
asking for a ride.
It's nineteen-
fifty-eight and
I'm yet
innocent to
many things.
I met
Mr. Carpenter at
our county fair.
He's older,
twenty-three,
I think.
He knows a
lot about
many things.
He is
interesting and
smart.
He likes me.
I'm only
seventeen, but
I believe he thinks
I'm also
interesting and
smart.
I let him in my car.

He suggests
we go to a
drive-in restaurant,
Treeanon,
it's called, for a
coke or something.
He says, "I'll buy."

We head out on
East Wabash with
car windows down,
letting warm
summer air
flow through car.

He buys
each of us a
coke and a
Treeanon famous
breaded
tenderloin sandwich.
We eat,
talk and laugh.
He tells great stories.
He expounds on some
interesting subject.
I'm amazed at
what all he knows.
My world is
expanding, yet
innocent to some degree.
My erudition is
about to get
more complicated.

Mr. Carpenter puts
his hand on

my leg and asks,
"Can I make you?"
I don't know
what that means.
"Can I give you a
blow job?"
He continues to
educate.
I answer,
"I don't think so."

He rubs and
pets me as if
I'm his girlfriend,
like I touch
my girlfriend,
Jackie, but
he wants to
go farther than
Jackie and
I ever do.
I have deep
respect for
Jackie and
never force
myself on her.
"Can I make you?"
he asks again.
"No,
I don't think so."
"Let's drive to
some place private,"
he says and
pushes onward
towards a place
I fear to go.
I say again,
"I don't think so."

My ears are hot;
my stomach wants to
throw up that
tenderloin sandwich.
He fondles me more.
I want to hit him,
push him out of
my car.
"Let me suck you,"
he insists.

"Get out of
my car"
I whisper,
"or I will slug you,"
I softly speak,
staring with
resolute eyes.
He doesn't listen,
but unzips
my pants,
pulls out
my penis and
starts to
go down on me.
Something in
my brain says,
let him do it and
something says,
throw him out.
I grab his shirt,
pull him upward,
squeeze his neck and
say, "Out, out."

I feel his neck skin
wrinkling within
my strong
farm boy hand.
I'm nearly crushing
his neck.
He pulls away,
looking at
my darkened face and
says nothing.
I also see my face
reflecting in a
small car
rearview mirror.
I see fear,
anger and
confusion.
He opens
his door and
lets himself out.

I sit still for
several minutes.
My camera mind is
already recording and
reviewing,
recording and
reviewing in silent
movie mode, but
it can't edit,
can't erase.
I slowly
drive home with
mind whirling.
He breaded,
deep-fried and
served an hour of

life to me.
It seems like a
big chunk of
innocence was
consumed as if a
tenderloin sandwich.

I want to
forget, but
mind has
permanently
recorded everything.
I play it back.
It reveals same
experience
every time.
Another organic
documenting
reel of Mr. Carpenter
is placed on
my mental
movie shelving.
My library is
getting bigger,
gaining time and
space, and
experiential weight.
My complicated mind
continues to
simply process like a
movie camera and
my silent soul
mortally collects like a
renowned
movie studio.

Golden Coin

Sometimes my mind wanders
past reality, into Hollywood grandeur,
into a short lifetime of splendor.
It's like I'm a storm waiter or a
disaster organizer,
expecting raw clouds to
make electricity that will
light my movie making way.

Trepidation roams ominous sky,
kissing with blackened lips and
caressing with lightning fingers.
I'm waiting and living like an
unfinished business villain.
Into pocket I reach for a
golden coin to purchase
more validating virgin film.

I find a smashed silver watch
instead that tells time no more.
I fear being a forged sword,
in sheath waiting for a hand.
But, in reality, I'm an organic
camera recorder of combat action, a
mind container of fast time past, a
soul collector of life experience lost.

o

Life was finding my illusive pathway,
seeking own accumulating identity and
making sense of an unfolding world.

Basketball

I see
Karen Jo Francis
leading a cheer,
twirling,
raising her long
cheerleader skirt with
just enough
centrifugal force to
show lower part of
her legs.
I see this while
preparing to
shoot a free throw.
I love playing in
my small intimate
warm gym, with
crowd about and
noise caressing
my mind.
I see an orange rim,
feel myself shooting
jump shots,
hook shots,
set shots and
layups.
It's here where
I developed
my jump hook and
step back set shot.

I see
my locker room where
I meticulously prepare for

battle, where
I meditate before
knowing meditation, where
I psych myself before
knowing psychology, where
I play mental movies of
past performances and
future successes.
Faces of Phil, Donnie, Steve,
Larry and Jerry flash as if
unfolding yesterday,
playing basketball.
There's no end to
melancholy provoking films.
I'm scouting myself.

3:30 P.M. Friday, January 9, 1959

In a small
gymnasium
filled with people
wishing me to play
basketball well, a
band plays,
cheerleaders yell as
I warm-up for
my last game.

.

I stretch a
bit more,
straighten socks and
tuck shirt well while
waiting for last
few shots before
informing horn
sounds.

I practice
outside set shots,
move closer for
jump shots and
then under basket for
power layups.
I move
outside again,
working up a
definite sweat,
then jab step,
shot fake,
crossover dribble and
jump shoot.
I go back inside,
do my invented
jump-hook.

I finally end
free throw shooting.
Everything is
going well.
I sink nearly
every shot.
My world is
here and now.
It is my last
high school game.

I see no future
past time left to
be a star in a
little world.
I don't realize
present reality is
disappearing.
New experiences

will too soon
invade mind and
change soul.
Filming essence
will never same
participate.

10:30 P.M. Sunday, January 11, 1959

I am a novel,
cask of wine,
bell tolling,
yet I fear
I will not
emerge as
worthy.

Does history
make a man, or
does a man
make history?
Either way,
I conjure a
strategy in
playful mind.

It's like dawn is
coming and
I fear light
will be in
short supply.
I then reason that
I must put fears
aside and gaze as
far as a mind can see.

Life By Itself

Sometimes
I can't sleep
in early
morning darkness.

Crazy words and
pictures float
from soul like
reminding light.

o

A cistern might be deep with
abundant fresh water, but
an old broken pump
cannot raise needed resource.

A fish full stream can supply
bait for a fisherman's tackle, but
by itself cannot provide
knowledge and wisdom.

Wheat cannot nourish by a
man's diligent thrashing and
grinding alone, but can by
silent use of fire provide bread.

An eager boy might be
blessed with strength, but
cannot willingly by himself
carry all occurring burdens.

o

Soft film
editing light at
three o-clock invites
vivid moving pictures.

If I live a
hundred years,
night awakening
will be a blessing.

Room is dark, yet
mind is light with
thoughts, ideas and
dream glowing plans.

In early morning
inviting darkness,
I can't help, but
remain awake.

o

Sometimes
I can't sleep
in early
morning darkness.

Crazy words and
pictures float
from soul like
reminding light.

The Bank

I'm walking through
Merchants National Bank
located at seventh and
Wabash Avenue in
Terre Haute during
nineteen fifty-nine year.
I see marble floors and
vertical metal bars
eight feet tall on
both lobby sides,
protecting tellers in
bank teller cages.
Bank president,
Mr. Carroll, is at
his desk, west side
up front, near brass
revolving and swinging
entrance doors.
He is talking,
shaking hands and
calling out names.
He is small, but
his voice is loud.
I hear him calling out for
his secretary all day long,
"Ramona, Ramona."
It is amusing to me.
She is small and looks
like Minnie Mouse with
her large lipstick mouth that
seems to never speak.
Opposite side, up front, is
Frank Hannish who is
essentially my boss.

I'm a messenger and
work in clearings, but
he keeps me busy delivering
courthouse abstracts.
He's grumpy and serious.
He's bald, yet has dandruff
on his black suit.
Mr. McConkey for
whom I also work and
run errands is talking to
Bill Weir at his teller cage.
Bill is smoking a cigar,
greeting and meeting people
while talking to bank manager
McConkey.
He has a great personality,
extroverted for sure.
He gives me advice
constantly.
I'm only eighteen.
He's thirty-five,
worldly and big city wise.
Sometimes we eat lunch
together at Millers pool hall.
He sometimes buys
us a cold beer.
I think Mr. Carroll would
disapprove of
us drinking beer at
lunchtime, especially
when I am under age and
we being frequently late.

9:00 A.M. Monday, December 14, 1959

I see myself a
few months later in a
teller cage with Madge.

She is teaching
me to be a teller and
we are getting along fine.
She is pretty,
well built and has a
great personality.
I like looking at her and
looking at our green money
filled drawers.
I have fantasies about
stealing some of it.
It's only paper while
I'm working,
putting it in and
out of money drawers,
counting, banding and
balancing totals; but
come payday when
I get my cash pay envelope,
it all looks very real.
I imagine what
I could do with it.
Madge is teaching
me how cool
it is to smoke.
We smoke right there
in our teller cage.
I practice at home.
It makes me sick, but
I continue to smoke.
In mirror I stare,
pretending maturity with
smoke getting in my eyes.
I think it's cool.
It's so James Dean.

10:00 A.M. Wednesday, January 20, 1960

Mr. Greene is dying
right before my eyes.
He is having a
heart attack and
no one really knows
what to do.
I do nothing, but
watch while someone
hovers over him,
loosening his tie,
speaking to him.
He doesn't respond.
He is turning red,
then white, then a
greenish color.
Mr. Greene is gone.
In created commotion,
I steal an inviting
hundred dollar bill from
our teller drawer.
I falsely count
our drawer money and
look for mistakes in
accounting numbers,
pretending to be concerned.
Madge and I have a little
slush fund, using it when
balancing our daily
cage transactions, and
if we're off balance
under a quarter,
we put in or take out
coins to make it balance.
We then vault roll our cart and

go home.
Today, of course,
we cannot balance.
We usually balance perfectly.
She is frustrated.
I am cool.
We cannot find a
mistake and I know why.
She trusts me explicitly.
She doesn't suspect that
I am a thief.
I don't feel
like a thief, but
I know I am a thief.
We finally chalk it up to a
transposition error,
locking up our cart and
vault rolling it.
I guess for now
I got away with robbery.
I guess forever that makes
me a bank robber.

4:00 P.M. Thursday, February 10, 1960

There is a man who walks
down an alley from
Roots Department Store
every day with a
gym bag full of
cash and checks,
heading for our bank to
deposit daily receipts.
I frequently fantasize about
knocking him unconscious,
stealing his money and
heading for California.

I also fantasize about
vault bank robbing, but that
seems a bit more difficult than
robbing an old
department store courier or
taking a hundred dollar bill.
I'm not a thief virgin
anymore and
I'm not proud of it.
I'm drifting into
unfamiliar territory here.

I'm recording
it all with vivid film and
resonating sound.
I'm a documentary on
how to chip away at
innocence,
nearly without awareness.
It's all here in
my mind, soul and spirit.
It's all in my memory,
wherever that resides.
My spiritual conscience is
working, but
my earthly flesh is
flirting with disaster.

o

I was an immorality accomplice,
ignorance held my hand while
innocence fell mysteriously silent.

Chapter IX

MARCH 1960						
Sunday	Monday	Tuesday	Wednesday	Thursday	Friday	Saturday
		1	2	3	4	5
6	7	8	9	10	11	12
13	14	15	16	17 St Patrick's Day	18	19
20	21	22	23	24	25	26
27	28	29	30	31		

Defining Modesty

It is more
than an it,
taking on energy,
life and stature.
It's a she, as if
having heart,
mind and soul.

She latently
mind flirts with
adolescent me,
resting lowly still,
shining and gleaming,
anxiously waiting to be
started and driven.

My Second Car

I picture
my second car
sitting in front of
my house, waiting
my attention and
admiration.
I call it
"The Tender Trap."
It's painted on
both tail fins in
small old English
lettering.

It is more
than an it,
taking on energy,
life and stature.
It's a she, as if
having heart,
mind and soul.
She latently
mind flirts with
adolescent me,
resting lowly still,
shining and gleaming,
anxiously waiting to be
started and driven.

She is a fifty-seven
turquoise and white
two door hardtop
fifty-seven Chevy.
She has a

two-hundred and
eighty-three
cubic inch block, with
Iskenderian
high-lift racing cam,
solid lifters and
two four-barrel
carburetors that
give her power and
confidence.
I can hear carburetors
sucking air and
solid lifters chattering.
I can hear and
emotionally feel
her engine loping.
It's music to my ears.

An eleven inch
truck clutch mates
her engine to a three speed
transmission with
Corvette floor shifter.
She is lowered
five inches,
front and back,
sitting about
four inches off pavement.
Her hood and
trunk are shaved,
leaded in and
painted to make
her look
clean and sleek.
A custom-made grill and
chrome reversed
wheels with

center spinners
make her unique.
Bigger and fatter
than stock tires
make her look
mean and tough.
Duel exhaust pipes
transiting into
four chrome
scavenger pipes
sticking out back
get her noticed.

I bend down on
each side of her to
unfasten chrome
gas caps,
sticking out behind
front tires.
They are open
straight pipes from
pickup truck
gas filler tubes welded to
header pipes.
I unfasten them
when cruising
around town or
when drag racing.
Some times
I uncap them for
only a few minutes,
only to make a
lot of engine noise.
Cops don't like them;
they're illegal exhaust.
Many times
I just sit around,

listening to my
engine lop at an idle.

She has white and turquoise,
rolled and tucked
naugahyde seats and
door panels,
white headliner and
new turquoise carpet.
I mind see her at
her best, but
she didn't get this
beautiful overnight.
It took a lot of
time and money to
make her uniquely
beautified.
I love my car.
I can look and
drive her all day and
night.

o

That is what
I movie see and hear;
that is what
I emotionally and
rationally feel.
I wish I could yet
today care for her,
not own, but
guardian her,
cherish her like a
woman, friend,
partner.

Heating and Cooling

Margret is a
real woman
who makes me feel
like a boy.
At nineteen,
I look and act
like a man, but
there's something
missing.
Maybe growing up
too fast,
becoming half a
man at ten years old
slowed maturation.
Maybe it's Father's
advice I hear
mind saying,
"Keep it in your pants
until you get married."

Margret is tall with
long brown hair and
long shapely legs.
She is exotic looking,
dark completed with
blues eyes,
my features in fact.

I'm not sure how, but
I find myself in
her faintly lit
bedroom,
soft pillows are

bed strewn,
soft comforter is
inviting and
odor is breathtaking.
Margret is wearing a
skimpy negligee,
motioning me to
come closer.

I go closer and
we become one.
She shows me how to
use a condom.
I'm moving in
unfamiliar territory.
I'm a virgin at
nineteen and
ignorant.
I mentally hear
my father say,
"Keep it in
your pants," but
his deep voice
fades as
Margret causes
my world to blur.
I'm falling in and
making love
all in one night.

I hear sounds.
She says,
"That's my father,
leaving for his
heating and
cooling business."

I reason that
I'm out of my element.
My family doesn't even
have a furnace,
much less an
air-conditioner.
I settle down,
remaining there until
her father
leaves for work,
before her mother
awakens and while
I'm yet in one piece.
She is too much
woman for me, yet
she wants more of
less boyish me.
I must get out of here.
I'm in over my
awe-inspired head

o

*There is more to tell about
my relationship with
Margret, but that
should remain covert and
on a back mental
movie shelf for now.*

Ditching Cops

I'm driving
my fifty-seven Chevy
on US Highway 41,
north of Farmersburg,
alongside a friend in
his fifty-five Chevy.

I play with
accelerating,
foolishly pushing
my finely tuned
machine to
sixty, sixty-five
then to seventy;
my friend stays beside.

We urge our cars to
ninety mph as
we near Highway 246;
then see a state trooper's
blue striped white car
approaching other side.

My friend
slams brakes,
turning East onto 246 while
I keep going straight,
seeing Mr. State Trooper
turning around.

I turn around in
next crossover and
we pass opposite

directions in
dim dusk light;
I nearly see
him scowling.

After passing,
I head South and
he heads North
turning around again,
following and
trying to catch me.

I turn West onto 246,
dousing lights;
it's now dark and
I can barely see, but
I cannot slow and
chance arrest.

Remembering that a
friend of my dad
lives a couple miles away;
I carelessly shoot-up
Delbert Turner's
driveway in darkness.

I steer next to
his car while
seeing a car with
red flashing lights
pass by quickly as
Delbert asks, "Who's there?"

I get out of my car,
explaining my situation,
standing in darkness.
Zoom, a

police car with
blinking lights goes by.

"Come inside and
have a cup of coffee."
Delbert says.
I follow him towards
his back door, and again zoom.
"He wants you bad."

Mr. Cop is certain that
I'm near that area, but
he can't find
sneaky me while
I remain at Delbert's for
more than an hour.

I'm off a risky hook
one more time;
being my third time
ditching cops,
knowing
I have to settle down.

I hear Father,
"You're going get in
big trouble someday."
I hear trooper Bovenshulty,
"We have to keep you
alive until you grow up."

I fear I'm not
maturing from
accelerating and
moving fast for
it seems in
my blood.

I remember
mother saying
long ago before
I began driving,
"I always wanted
to be a racecar driver."

o

Little did I know
how stupid
I was until
later in life
I helicopter watched
cop ditching
on TV and then
realized how
dangerous were
my illegal actions.

Defining

A psychology
professor is
telling me that
one cannot
remember
earlier than
five years of age.
I tell him that
I can remember
when being a baby and
much before
two years old.

He dismisses me,
saying, "It's impossible."
One other student
wishes to argue,
saying she can also
remember some things.
He dismisses us again, but
we know
earlier pictures and
feelings later
get names and
definitions.

I'm very mental,
visually acute and
have been forever,
believing everything
experienced is
mind accumulated and
later soul stored.

I later learn to
define and classify
everything.
I'm a self-made movie star
filming own memory.

o

I am a
wonderful creation.
God gave
me wonderful
tools, like
mind, eyes and
ears, like
heart, stomach and
lungs, like
hands, arms and
legs, but
soul is best.

o

I life came to experience.
I school learned to reason.
I worked career to earn.
I wisdom wrote to teach.
I heaven returned to report.

Chuck

Chuck Walker and
I are Republican National
Convention watching.
He's standing and
shouting for
Berry Goldwater's
nomination.
We're both Young
College Republican
members.

His apartment is a mess,
clothes scattered
everywhere,
sink full of
dirty dishes and an
engine block
sitting in living
room middle.
His apartment is
chaos, but
his mind is precise and
manners orderly.
He dresses
immaculately in shirt,
tie and suit.
He's a dichotomy,
inside and out.
Chuck works at
Roots Department Store
in men's clothing.
He selected me for
Roots College Board.

It's an inside job,
cronyism,
I think it's called.

4:00 P.M. Saturday, August 27, 1960

We are escorting a
Playboy bunny
to and from airport and
promotional events at
Roots store.
College Board
work is tough, but
we love it,
hoping Miss July of
1957 will
like us, but
she is all business.
We just mostly
look at her,
trying to be cool while
imagining possibilities.
I subtly give her
my best James Dean
impression.

Mother Louise

If sweetness
could pave roads to
success, then
my mother,
Mary Louise,
would have a
super highway
on which to
drive her new
shiny car.

She was
tiny, about a
hundred pounds,
before
my brother was born.
She is now
no taller, but
somewhat rounder.
She yet laughs and
giggles like a
school girl.

She wished
city girl
living, but
ended up
country woman
thriving.
She wished
race car
driving, but
ended up

Plymouth sedan
cruising.

Oh, how well
we dream of
things that
might be and
end up with
things that are
just plain loving,
like God,
family and
country.

I owe her much.
She timely gives
gentleness and
grace, for
I want little, but
when needed,
she soothes
my soul.

She calls me
her "rock," but
I am only a
family stone,
found and
polished by
her patience.

She doesn't say,
"I love you," but
love drapes
my mind,
body and
soul.

I know
she loves me
no matter what,
unconditionally,
gracefully.
What else
do I as a
growing boy
want or need?
What else
will I as a
grown man
some day
want or need?

o

Mary Louise died in
her bed one night at
seventy nine years old
with a slight smile, or
so said a friend who
found her next day.
She had gone to the
beauty parlor that day to
get her hair fixed.
I think she mowed
her lawn the day before.
She lived alone and
loved it that way, but
visited much and
kept many friends close.

Keedy and The Kats

"Keedy and The Kats" are
on stage at an old
theater converted into a
nightclub called,
The Idaho Club.
I walk into
near darkness,
stepping down from
bar area into
lower level with
tables and
chairs placed
close together.
Small lights
on tables flicker.
I see familiar faces.
Don and
Chuck are here, and
Jon, my gang.
Further down is
Keedy and
his band playing.
I'll talk to him later.

I'm nineteen and
illegally coming here for
three months.
Drinking age is
twenty-one.
Most everything is
allowed in Terre Haute:
underage drinking,
bribery, gambling,

prostitution.
There are slots,
roulette tables and
cards upstairs.
Some call Terre Haute
"sin city."
I think Mayor
Ralph Tucker
calls it opportunity.
I think he gets a
piece of all action.

9:00 P.M. Saturday, December 4, 1960

Keedy is a
drummer from
Indianapolis with a
rock and roll band of
five musicians.
He's stocky with
strong arms from
nightly banging on
drums for hours.
He is doing a
twenty minute drum solo
during a song called,
"Caravan."
He's getting a
lot of attention.
Other band
members are gone,
leaving him on stage
alone to play and
sweat over his drums.
A watching crowd
loves him, but
he's getting too much

attention.
I overhear
club manager,
Bob, say,
"It's too long.
People aren't drinking.
I'm losing money.
Tell him to cut it to
five minutes."

11:00 P.M. Saturday, December 4, 1960

I'm here not for
drinking, but for
music listening.
I also sneak into
other clubs to
listen to music.
I love to slowly
drink beer and
intently listen to
rock and roll music.
I have a
great time at
The Idaho Club,
Sixth Avenue and
The Spot.

The Spot is nearly
my favorite.
It's a small bar
across from
Sixth Avenue.
It's in a triangular
shaped building at a
corner where two
angling streets intersect.

It's where a
black man named
Boone Dunbar plays a
rock organ.
He plays with
his usual drummer and
saxophone player.
I never hear music
like Boone's music
anywhere else.
It's certainly
unique in
nineteen-sixty.

o

Rumor had it that
Boone's sax man
played with Duke Ellington
for a short time
until one tragic day
they brought out
new sheet music and
he couldn't read it.
He had memorized all of
Duke's recorded music and was
getting along just fine
until that verifying day.
He was a great
saxophone player, but
Duke said he needed to
read music to play
successfully in his band.

I'm No Secret

No Eastwood Club
gambling or music is
playing here tonight out
on East Wabash Avenue.
It's next to a, best in
town, hamburger place.
We stop for a burger,
then Eastwood Club visit.
It's nearly empty,
only long bar,
tables and chairs,
few people present.
No usual poker,
blackjack or
roulette tables, and
no slots present.
There is no back room
high stakes
poker game happening.
Tip-offs and
protection bribes are
no secret here.
Raids and police
crackdowns are
no secret either, but
I'm a secret
like slots and
roulette tables
because at nineteen,
I am also not here.

All Grind

Upon miller's
bright idea
I jump to
grind and
pulverize, and
something useful
make, like
grain into flour.
With rough mind
I grind ideas and
something useful
make, like
something sweet and
intelligent bake.

I grow such
ideas to
convert, gather and
compile.
I'm becoming a
stone wheel
grinder with
no regard for
fear or
conscience.
"Good for me"
seems a
worthy business.

Chapter X

JULY 1961

Sunday	Monday	Tuesday	Wednesday	Thursday	Friday	Saturday
						1
2	3	4 Independence Day	5	6	7	8
9	10	11	12	13	14	15
16	17	18	19	20	21	22
23	24	25	26	27	28	29
30	31					

Feeling
Maturity

I am warily treading
in a suspicious sea of
agitated dreams.

Quiet maturity hold
my trembling hand,
spiritually lead me
beyond present
lacking awareness.

Maturity

I surely seek you,
"Maturity," with your
hidden signs placed
along paths crawled,
walked and driven.
How is it that you
forever circumvent
my grasping mind?
Could it be that
I have not sought
you well as might?
On tipping point,
I fear failure lurks
this awakening day.
I have a bad taste
in dry mouth and
bad thoughts in
vulnerable head.
I am warily treading
in a suspicious sea of
agitated dreams.
Quiet maturity hold
my trembling hand,
spiritually lead me
beyond present
lacking awareness.

Don

*Sometimes
I am provoked to
call up multiple
movies,
movies of people
left behind, but
not forgotten.*

o

Don Williams is
sitting next to me in
my first college class.
He says he is
ex-Navy.
"I'm in the Navy
Reserve," I inform.
"I was in the
real Navy," he explains.
"I have two years of
active duty to serve
one of these days,"
I retort.
"Ok, that's
good enough."

We become
instant friends,
friends for life.
We study little
together,
drink some
together,

drive cars much
together and
plan to go to
California some day.

Don is six feet three,
big boned and
muscular.
I am six feet one,
athletic and
strong as hell.
Our friend Jim is
six feet,
big and tough.
Jon Thomas is
five feet four,
small and quiet.
He says,
"I always feel safe
with you guys."
We three big guys are
suspiciously
going to college.
Jon bakes cookies and is
happy so doing.

College

I am learning what
I want, not
what they want.
I love learning,
discovering and
thinking.
It is exciting.
Too bad,
I can't write
my own syllabus,
pick own classes,
decide own major.
I'm getting poor grades,
majoring in business,
frankly thinking
it might be discipline or
concentration lack.
Maybe I don't know
how to study,
never had to before.
Everything used to be
easy in high school.
I made good grades.

My friend Chuck
figures to
never graduate and
if he does,
he will be fifty years old.
I don't think about
graduating for
I can't see
distant goals.

My dad explains
peg placing,
driving towards, then
placing another peg.
It sounds simple,
seems complicated.
I'm moment living
in good times.

I'm afraid
Uncle Sam is
shaping futures,
drafting for
Viet Nam.
My number is
getting close.
Nonetheless,
Chuck and I are
on campus and into
social life for now.
We are also
mixing and
mingling with
campus girls.
That's our major.

I see us at
Uncle Dr. Vogus's
house drinking
free beer and
visiting with
Chuck's cousin.
We go there
frequently to
say hello and
drink some beer.
Doc has house parties,
we invite ourselves.

I never see
Chuck blind drunk.
I've been that way
one time by
sheer accident.
We don't drink much
because we
can't afford it and
I'm a poor drinker,
having a small
bladder and thus
peeing often.
I traverse from
table to restroom
all night
after two beers.
Sometimes
I dance and
sweat, rather than
traverse and pee.

College seems
my minor and
life my major.
Music and
barhopping are
my college
distractions.
I can't see
past today and
I fear tomorrow
will show
me another
way to live.

Janie O'Rourke

Two large
stone pillars with
opened iron gates,
funnel my car from
street to narrow
driveway
leading to campus.
A campus police officer is
signaling for
me to stop.
He asks
my business and
without answer,
says, "Park on the
Boulevard."
I know his words and
routine well.
I am at St. Mary-of-the-
Woods College,
an all
girls' school.
I have been here
many times.
I know his
advising words.
He tells everyone,
"Park on the boulevard."
I park, walk into a
dormitory and
take basement
stairs down to where
"Woods" girls come to
meet boys.

It is handy
because if a guy
wants to meet girls or
find a new friend,
he comes here.
I join in,
seeing people
I know as
guys and girls
basement roam,
meeting and greeting,
looking for
someone to love.

I see a girl
near far wall,
talking to another girl.
I approach,
introduce myself, and
suddenly I am
in love with
Janie O'Rourke.
She is from Queens,
New York City, that
in itself is interesting.
She has a
New York accent, but
says New Yorkers
believe she has a
Midwestern accent.
She is small,
cute and smart.
We soon hit it off.

I date Janie for
several months.
Then inevitably

I need greener
pastures to roam,
past basement,
past campus.
I yet seek worldly
views, new spaces.

o

I reluctantly went
basement hunting
after we broke up, but
I was never
successful in
finding love again.
I finally quit
boulevard parking,
basement searching,
St. Mary-of-the-
Woods dating.

Route 66

Don, Jon and
I are driving on a
famous highway,
leading us
towards a
final destination, a
California beach.
Route 66 is
evoking anticipation
in heart while
mind turns
faster than
my fifty-seven
Chevy wheels.
We are living
television;
Route 66 is
in our blood and
beneath our
mobile feet.
I mind provoke
TV episodes of
"Route 66."
We stop for gas,
pee and eat.
Driving is
our thing and
California is
our goal.
I hear my dad's
peg placing voice
speaking, and
begin to value

his philosophy.
My goal,
my peg is
Hollywood.

A mechanic in
Kansas
won't install a
new fuel pump.
He says my engine is
too hot and
won't do anything
until tomorrow.
I look at Don.
He says,
"I don't know how."
Jon says,
"I'm not mechanical."
Mr. Gas Station explains
how to change a
fuel pump.
I can't wait for
tomorrow, next peg or
California coast.
I change it,
burning blisters on
hands and arms, but
it is done and
we are on our
sojourn again.
I set another goal,
place another peg,
rack another movie.

We drive across hot
Mohave Desert
landscape with

windows up to
stay cool.
We finally reach
Los Angeles,
Sunset Boulevard,
Twentieth Street and
Vine.
I am cruising
Hollywood.
I am high on
goals and pegs
conquered.
I am high on
life.

We stay in
Hollywood for
two days, don't get
discovered or robbed;
so we head south
towards Long Beach,
towards an ever
new tomorrow.

o

Long Beach wasn't a
big city in 1962 and
we easily sought
living space, jobs,
mischief and beaches.
California was my first,
"Great Adventure," but
certainly not my last.

California Sun

I'm driving
southward,
heading towards
Long Beach.
Sunshine warms skin,
cool morning air
tickles arm and
brushes face as
I lean out of a
downed window.

Small Long Beach
seems tame
compared to
big, bad,
rebellious
Los Angeles.
We track down a
friend summer
visiting
her aunt in
Long Beach.

We find an
apartment and
soon run out of
money and
get jobs.
I work at
Paley's,
Don repos
cars and
John washes

dishes.
Life is good
on a sunny
California beach.
We're working,
laughing and
drinking.
I like my job,
Don hates his and
Jon doesn't care.
Huntington Beach is
our favorite place to
hang out while
swimming,
sun bathing and
grunion hunting.
Summer is passing
too quickly.

10:00 A.M. Sunday, July 15, 1962

We're in
Tijuana, Mexico
getting my car
white naugahyde
tucked, rolled and
pleated with new upholstery.
Two sweaty women
constantly sew and
two tough men
install leather while
we Tijuana
hang out.
We curiously return
every few hours,
checking progress.
It takes

eighteen hours, but
final result is
beautiful.
We haggle price.
Don pretends to
find faults and
Chico takes
fifty dollars less.
Everyone is
happy.
Chico offers
sewing women
sex for ten dollars.
We say,
"No thanks," but
buy five liters of
Tequila instead and
head back towards
Long Beach.
We smuggle it
across border,
deciding later,
no one cares.
We spend
fifty dollars
trying to make
it drinkable.
No one likes
Tequila except
our landlady.

10:00 A.M. Monday, August 6, 1962

Soon it's time to
Indiana return.
Leaving
beautiful girls and

inviting beaches is
difficult and
Indiana seems
far away.
We finally find
discipline for
first time
all summer and
pack our bags.

I buy four
chrome-reversed
wheels with
center spinners for
my car
just before leaving.
I've been
admiring them
all summer.
They are final
transforming parts for
my awesome
driving machine.
I can't wait,
returning home and
showing it off.

1:00 P.M. Thursday August 6, 1962

Kid part in me
is ever active.
I yet feel
California sun and
beach breezes, and
see Los Angeles
gleaming and
Long Beach

reflecting as
summer films
play in
my head.
I long to return,
sometimes wishing
I had never left.

o

Paley's was a precursor for the
modern department store.
It was kind of like
Home Depot and Pier One
all in one subdivided store.
It was way ahead of its time.
They offered me an
assistant manager's job because
I was smart and worked hard.
It was so new and interesting to
me that I couldn't help but
have passion for my job.

Naval Reserve

I see a
gray Naval
Reserve Center
out east of
Terre Haute.
I then see Seybold
brothers in
khaki summer
Navy uniforms,
explaining reserve
requirements and
training.
They drive
eighty miles from
northern Indiana
once a month for
weekend meetings.
They say,
"You will serve
six years
minimum,
two years active,
one week-end a
month and
two weeks
during summer."
I will be a
Communications
Technician.

It sounds
better than
Uncle Sam

drafting me.
There are rumors
concerning
Viet Nam
looming and that
means war.
I want no
part of war.
Cold War is
good enough for
me.
I don't want
to be a hero.

I will be FBI
investigated and
will receive a
Top Secret
security clearance,
serving on a
need to know
basis and
essentially be an
electronic spy.
I will indirectly
work for NSA as
cheap labor,
collecting
information from
foreign
governments and
militaries that are
US enemies.

I will serve at any
one of many
Naval Security

Group Activities
worldwide,
but not on a ship.
Ninety-five percent of
all field work
accomplished by
NSG is done from
land bases.
I have a little
problem with
motion sickness
so that is good news.
I sign-up with
Seybold brothers
swearing me in and
figuratively
hold my hand.

High Hanging Fruit

I reach for goals as if
they are fruit on
low hanging branches,
easy to grasp and
into sink teeth.

I wish sweet juices to
drip from mouth and yet
I cannot reach best,
mediocre disappoints,
dry and bland seeming.

Why can't such fruit
mark my path,
lie beneath my feet or
be willingly to drop
from branches high?

I hope I don't have to
climb high into life's
tangled hierarchy to
obtain sweetest
love and joy fruit.

o

I used to entertain thoughts
concerning setting goals and
achieving goals, then came along
old age, and I gave up a seeking and
adopted an accepting philosophy.

Out of Control

I see myself in
film projector light,
balancing between
failure and success.
I am studying less,
drinking more and
see myself as
surely mediocre.

I have no
girlfriend, only a
few friends and
no ambition.
I am living with
my parents and
spending my last savings
on only myself.
I am guilty of
free loading.

My grade point
average is below
two points.
I am brink standing,
nearly being asked to
leave college and
I don't care.
I am bored being a
business major and
want to fly and
not classroom sit.
Professors are boring,
subjects are useless and
campus is too small.

I keep pushing
towards an
unacceptable line,
sometimes moving
beyond it,
being careless,
gambling with
my life.
If not for luck,
some discipline, and
my father's
conscience voice
speaking in
my head,
I would be in
jail or dead.

I am teetering
on disaster,
skating on
thin ice,
walking a
proverbial
tight rope.
I am out of
control and
know it.
I wish to change,
reset goals,
grow up and
further chip away at
dubious innocence.

I wish to
fly away on a

big airplane to
new places and
new things.
I wish new ideas,
thoughts and
experiences.
I wish a waiting
future, not
floundering in
old movies
presently playing
in my head.

I wish new
movies to
generate new
Phil images.
I wish to
learn about
self and
act out poetic
words and
moving pictures
flashing in
my head.
I need to go
worldly and
have maturity
transform my boyish
essence.

o

I walk outwardly,
live inwardly.
My unique world is
only here because

I affirm its existence.
Reality is illusion
in mind from
affecting experience.
True self is a
long time
spiritual being
occupying a
short time
earthly body.
Mind movies in
my head are thus
spiritual movies in
my soul.

o

I die for a moment
when I sneeze.
My heart stops,
brain seeks and
mind wonders.
I fly a universal path to
heaven and back,
learning knowledge
given in time's flash.
I know when a
sneeze is coming,
I prepare for
my departure and with
open mind
I come and go
without effort.
In sneezing,
I have no control
except to accept and
benefit.

12:30 P.M. Friday, November 22, 1963

John Kennedy

I see library steps
before me in
orderly fashion as
I descend towards
campus center,
towards a green
quadrangle area
full of people in
small groups
conversing.

There are few
steps, but
I middle step
stop as a girl says,
"They shot
President Kennedy."
I am motionless,
standing still for
several seconds,
dry mouth listening.
"Someone shot him."

Another piece of
innocence is
chipped away.
Mental disorder
shortly muddles
thoughts.
I know not of
shooting and
killing a president
except Lincoln.

I realize
I am naïve and
cannot move as
thoughts attack.
I cannot picture.
I finally reach
level sidewalk and
grassy quadrangle,
heading towards
Student Union.

I work my way
through people,
standing and
watching a
small black and
white television set.
I scarcely hear
Walter Cronkite
sorrowfully explaining
what happened.

He speaks of Dallas,
Texas on Friday,
November 22, 1963,
reporting what is
happening.
I stand alone in a
silent crowd with
noisy minds.
No one speaks
except Walter.

I turn to exit
dimly lit lounge,
wading through crowd,

shuffling feet,
wishing to be alone.
I play Kennedy films
in my head,
seeing him as
he was and not what
he is now, dead.

o

I play own movies of
that day and watch
re-recorded movies of
that day in my head.
They blend in melancholy
remembrance of the,
"Sixties," and all
that went on during
that tumultuous time.
Oh, how I grew during
that sixties time.
Oh, how I chipped away at
that innocence effortlessly.

Chapter XI

Sunday	Monday	Tuesday	Wednesday	Thursday	Friday	Saturday
1	2	3	4	5	6	7
8	9	10	11	12	13	14
15	16	17 St Patrick's Day	18	19	20	21
22	23	24	25	26	27 Passover begins at sunset	28
29 Easter	30	31				

www.PocketCalendar.com

Flaunting Liberation

"How come Navy guys
fly and Army guys take
ships coming over here?"

I shrug and say,
"I have no idea," but
I do know why.
I am NSG, and
I'm special.

Bainbridge, Maryland

Planes, trains and
buses finally bring
me to Bainbridge,
Maryland for
Communications
Technician school.

Afternoon sunlight smarts
my eyes as I pass
through guarded gates,
heading towards assigned
base barracks.
I find a bunk,
settle in a
dormitory while
thinking about
next day and
first day of school.
My fourteen week
accelerated school is
normally
twenty-six weeks.

7:00 A.M. Monday, March 9, 1964

I am part of a group of
sixty young men from
East Coast and Mid-west.
Most have at least
two years of college,
don't excessively
drink or gamble,
like music and athletics, and

are above average intelligence.
We are very much
alike through process of
elimination and
final FBI investigation for a
Top Secret clearance.

We seem profiled.
By world assignment time,
we will be all very similar,
even though White, Black,
Hispanic and Asian from
North, South,
East or West.
We are all between
twenty and twenty-five
years of age.

Our class begins with
sixty students, will
end with twenty-one of
which twelve will get
clearances and make it to
scattered parts of world.
Four of us will be truly
successful in a real world of
electronic spying that
allows few mistakes.

9:00 A.M. Monday, April 13, 1964

We receive
Morse code in
groups of five
encrypted letters in
ten groups per line and
ten lines per test.

Each letter consists of a
combination of short
"dit" and long
"da" sounds.
We will receive increasing
groups per minute.
We begin by learning
dits and das for
each English letter,
four extra Russian
alphabet letters, then
copy at a rate of two
groups per minute.
We increase speed after
passing tests near perfectly and
thus moving on to
another speed.
Fourteen groups
per minute is a
milestone rate and a
nerve-racking process.
Rumor tells us that is
where many students
flunk out.

11:00 P.M. Sunday, May 10, 1964

I see myself on a
three-day pass in
Greenwich Village,
visiting with
Janie O'Rourke.
She is showing
me around
New York City.
We are having a
great time,

remembering
St. Mary's,
dating and
Terre Haute.
She has one more
year of school.
I have two
years of service.

We are near
making love in
my hotel room on
my last night, but
Janie is Catholic and is
determined to remain a
virgin until married.
I respect that and
back off.
I will not force her to
do anything against
her will.
We finally part
early next morning
after sleeping
next to each other
all night.

"I will never
see you again,"
I say, knowing
it is probably true.
"Maybe when you
get back,
you can look me up,"
she says with
little conviction.

I return to
Bainbridge and
never see Janie again.

o

I can yet play a silent movie of
visiting Janie in Greenwich Village;
faintly see her fair face,
her brownstone house and
us on a crowded subway train.

Pressure

We are losing students
every week,
flunking out or
dropping out from
pressure put upon us to
do perfect work.
I enter fourteen groups a
week ahead and
finally pass a
week behind.
I am a nervous wreck by
fourteen groups per minute
code passing time.
I am determined to
finish code school.

It is smooth sailing
after fourteen groups.
We are down to
twenty-one students now,
nearing graduation.
To this point,
we have been listening to
machine generated
Morse code.
Our instructor sends us,
through our headphones,
real man made code in
real field conditions.
There is noise, static and
poorly sent code.
I understand hardly
any of it correctly.

I am scared that
I will fail when put in a
real situation, but
after a few days
I learn to tune out
extraneous noise and
listen only to code.
It is becoming
easy again.

9:00 A.M. Sunday, June 21, 1964

I am graduating,
being assigned to
Bremerhaven,
Germany and
have received
my Top Secret
clearance.
Fourteen weeks later
from entering,
I am excited with a
diploma in hand,
heading home for
two weeks and then
I shall fly to Germany.

10:00 A.M. Sunday, July 5. 1964

Liberation

I am sitting in a
two-engine
prop airplane with
engines idling,
propellers quietly
chopping air,
pilot waiting final
taxi permission
towards runway.

I see my parents and
little brother,
Warren,
standing behind a
chain link fence,
watching my airplane.
I look through a
small porthole, and
am sure they
cannot see me.
Mother is crying,
Dad gazing
outward as if in
deep thought while
Warren is smiling,
imagining going
with me, I suspect.

I feel same time
happy and sad,
nearly feeling
guilty for leaving
them behind.

Airplane is
waiting, but
I think all hell is
about to
break loose as
loud engines are
high rpm revving.
Whole airplane is
vibrating and
shaking with
brakes choked.
It's pulling and
straining against
itself as if
begging to be
released.

Propellers are
deafening.
I am scared
it's going to
fall apart.
This is all
new to me.
I keep looking for
nuts and
bolts to fall
all around me, but
none do.

10:15 A.M. Sunday, July 5, 1964

Someone finally
liberates my airplane,
allowing it to
lurch forward,
shaking

violently, and
then, like magic,
I feel it
leave earth.
Smooth air
lifts it upward,
vibration abates,
gravity pulls me
deeper in my seat.
I am excited and
scared, but
feel like an eagle.
Freedom suits me.

It is as if
I am also being
un-choked and
liberated,
lurched forward into
future realm.
I am excited for
I am first leg heading
towards Europe and
places beyond.
I am on that
dreamed of airplane,
taking me towards
new days, ways and
fatherland spaces.

I am eager to
film and record
new experiences.
I am becoming a
treasure chest of
vivid films,
capturing now for

future viewing.
I am heading for
maturity and
wisdom.
First time in life,
I am separating
from childhood ties
through time and
distance.

o

So much of what I now remember
seems like a dream or another life, except,
I have Kodachrome pictures to provoke
mind movies and prove my adventures.

Last Seat Taken

I am at
McGuire Air Force
Base, sitting and
waiting for an
overseas flight at
5:00 P.M.
Time moves slowly,
anticipation sparks
mind reflections.
Subtle thoughts
engage organic
mind imaging
machine.

I am finally
boarding,
beginning a quarter
mile walk towards a
Boeing 707 waiting.
Several boarding
military dependants
also seek same
skyward sojourn as me.
A lady, child and
newborn pass
with me through a
final gate and
onto tarmac.
I offer to carry
something.
She hands me
her baby nestled in a
portable seat.

Our airplane is far,
my arms are tired,
holding a baby with
forearms extended.
I understand
her needing help.
She explains that
she is joining her
Army officer husband
in Germany.

7:30 P.M. Monday, July 6, 1964

Boeing 707's are
enormous,
comfortable seats
galore.
I remain next to
mother and
children,
getting settled,
thinking about
Germany.

"Sir, you'll have to
find another seat.
Babies need
their own seat
during takeoff and
landing," a
civilian
contracted
Military Air
Transport Service
stewardess tells me.
"MATS airplane
rules."

I stand,
looking down
what must be
two hundred
filled seats.
"No empties,"
my stewardess
reports.
"I'm sorry,
you'll have to
take a later
flight."

I give up
my seat,
giving baby
one last look,
wondering if
he's recording and
filming like
I did when
three months old.

9:00 A.M. Tuesday, July 7, 1964

I am next day
another flight
waiting,
wondering if
next plane is
meant to be.
Maybe one
will crash.
Is it today's or
tomorrow's

airplane that is
doomed?
I am safe now, but
is next flight
ill fated?

I have no
control either way.
I can't worry, yet
creative thoughts
haunt while
idling time and
supposing.
I dismiss
useless thoughts,
watching airplanes
take off and land.

7:00 P.M. Tuesday, July 7, 1964

I see white clouds
far below through
airplane window,
then soon see
blue sky above,
blue ocean below.
It's like I doubt
whether I am
up or down.
I'm surrounded by blue.
Gravity, however,
distinguishes,
giving direction,
making foolish
sense of it all.

My second
airplane is a
slow moving
four engine
turboprop,
It stops in
Greenland for fuel
after several
flight hours.
I see two sunrises in
twenty-four hours,
flying up and
over Earth,
not around,
towards Frankfort,
Germany.
It takes
twenty-four
hours to get there,
six time zones plus
eighteen flight hours.
Home is far away,
for sure.

I calculate
trip home
in a Boeing 707
by subtracting
time zones from
seven flight hours.
Going home will
take one hour.
It plays with
my mind.
Times zones are
tricky.

7:00 P.M. Thursday, July 9, 1964

I am excitement full.
My seemingly
lumbering
turboprop airplane
softly Frankfort
Air Force Base lands.

7:00 P.M. Friday, July 10, 1964

I am train heading
towards North Sea,
towards Bremerhaven,
Germany and
Naval Security
Group Activity.

I'm in my fatherland,
grandfather's old country.
He arrived in America
when eight years old.
Grandfather seemed
wholly American, but
deep down inside,
he was very German.

In a strange way,
I feel at home.
Investigation of
German heritage
spawns imagination,
pride and
belonging sense.
It's like my
CT school instructor
instilling pride by

speaking of Naval
history,
Naval Security Group
creation and
WW II success.
I am mostly
German, but feel
completely German,
now here in Germany.
I wonder how
experiencing and
filming now will
affect me later.

o

It took me a long time to
get to Bremerhaven.
Airplane, train and
bus carried me towards
my new home.
I fondly remember that
place after being there for
two years.

NSGA

I see my new home as
I pass through
Military Police
guarded gates onto an
Army transportation
battalion base,
previously a WW II
German Air Force Base,
now in a British
controlled sector.
My bus moves along a
street circling a huge
grassy field to my left,
lined by tall trees and
many large red brick
buildings to my right.
Everything in town and
on base is clean.
I find out later that
it rains a lot.
Rain cleans and
greens frequently.
We pass a sign that
reads NSGA and
then stop at a building
labeled Administration.
"This is it gentlemen."
Our German bus driver
announces in good English.

9:15 A.M. Monday, July 12, 1964

An Army solder asks
while bus departing,
"Did you just come over
on a MSTS ship?".
I say, "No, I flew over."
"Really?" he questions.
"How come Navy guys
fly and Army guys take
ships coming over here?"
I shrug and say,
"I have no idea," but
I do know why.
I am NSG, and
I'm special.
That's what they told
us when signing up, at
every reserve meeting, at
CT school and
when receiving our
Top Secret clearance.

They say we are
top two percent Navy.
I think it's "bullshit," and
only a motivational tool for
getting us to do
near perfect work.
Maybe it's because
ninety-five percent of
what we do is
internationally illegal or
maybe it's because
we have secrets and
need protection.

"Those Russians would
love to get their hands
on you.
There are two thousand
full-time or part-time
spies in Bremerhaven.
Wear your uniform for the
first month and always
travel in twos,"
they tell us first day.

9:30 A.M. Monday, July 1964

Administration checks
me in and assigns a
room in one of many
nearby dormitories,
my new home.
I notice a Nazi swastika
yet inlaid in each brick
dormitory end wall.
I walk up several steps;
pass through large wooden
oak doors and into a hall
leading towards two stories of
identical rooms.

Eight men in each room, a
hundred rooms and
one recreational lobby
make up my new home.
There are four bunk beds,
eight lockers and
two windows.
Showers are down a
long hall to my left.

9:45 A.M. Monday, July 12, 1964

A short dark skinned
sailor dressed in dungarees,
Henry Dunbar,
points to an empty
bunk and locker.
That's yours,"
he says softly.
I nod.

o

I have many pictures
in my closet, but
even more movies
in my head.
Henry, Joe, Ron,
Al and Vennie, to
mention a few, are
old friends that
come to movie mind.
They speak to me as do
many others who I can see, but
not remember their names.
They all easily provoke
cinema action today for
I yet miraculously see
better than I faintly hear.

Vinnie and Al

I see Vennie and Al
downtown Bremerhaven, at
NSGA work spaces and at
our ex-Nazi dormitory.
Al plays pool well and
bowls great.
He is heavy, but has a
feather touch with a
pool cue and bowling ball.
Vinnie mostly talks and
I love to hear him speak.
They are both from
Rhode Island and
know each other
from early childhood.
They speak with a thick
Eastern accent and
I am beginning to
gain an accent of my own.
I'm also trading words,
for example,
soda for coke and
downtown for uptown.

We work, live and
play together.
Al is teaching
me how to
bowl correctly.
I am getting
much better, but
I don't think I can
teach him how to

play basketball.
Al wants to be a
professional gambler.

Vinnie has no idea
what he wants to be.
I align ambitions with
Vinnie, for all
I want to do is
grow up more,
get back home alive and
find a college major.

o

"Hey, Reis,
you want to
hat up and
head
downtown?"
I hear Vinnie
ask with that
Rhode Island
accent.
I wish to hear
him say that
again and
see both
my pals,
Al and Vennie,
again.

Fallen Stone

Dislodged stones
eventually cliff fall,
landing awkwardly
while others linger
temporarily lodged,
remaining gracefully
without purpose in
silent inertness.

Monuments cannot
themselves change
their destiny because
stone will not cry,
moan or rebel from
being engraved,
time weathered and
face clean eroded.

Some day
someone will
probably select a
stone on a path for
each of us,
be we good,
bad or
purposeful.

Perhaps it will be
placed near a
grassy path as
opposed to a
shifting mountain
fallen stone that is

scattered by
earthly energy.

All stones have
certain value and
precious ones are
coveted, yet
even three
million year old
diamonds succumb
one way or another.

Sooner or
later everything
falls, crumbles and
cliff falls,
becoming Earth's
headstone again in
purposeful repose with
God's intention.

o

*A poetic voice speaks to me as
movies are born in my creative head
no matter where I shortly reside.*

Nazi Bar

John Dace and
I are in a small
Downtown bar at
Two A.M. tipsy.
We started at
10:00 P.M.
Saturday night.

We get drunk,
Sober up,
Eat bratwurst and
Wash them down with
More beer.
I can't remain awake.
Dace is fine.

I hear commotion,
Look around and
See a German
Standing with
Outstretched
Right arm,
Nazi saluting.

He says, "Heil Hitler."
I ignore him.
Another stands
Clicks heels,
Yells, "Sieg Heil!"
I look at Dace.
He says, "No problem."

Two more, then
Two more,
Hitler salute and
Click heels.
I whisper, "Dace,
We're in a
Nazi bar."

Everyone then stands,
Saluting Hitler,
Looking Nazi like,
Staring at us.
Dace retorts,
"Let's get the fuck
Out of here."

"Say no more,"
I whisper distinctly.
"I guess when
They drew the
Iron curtain line,
All Nazis weren't in
East Germany."

Discipline

I am lifting
weights,
same time
every other day.
I lose partners
who cannot
keep schedules,
be dependable or
stand pain.

I pump iron with
vengeance,
seeking
physical and
mental strength.
Weight lifting
pushes me to
surpass
what I think is
impossible.

Seems when
reaching total
fatigue point,
thinking more
bench presses or
arm curls are
impossible,
I do one or
two more.

Amazingly,
I push

onward past
quitting point,
like survival
training,
surpassing
hardship and
despair.

I believe
it will save
my life
somehow.
I learn
lessons
lifting weights,
doing
impossible feats.

11:55 P.M. Monday, May 10, 1965

I'm in work
dungaree shirt,
denim pants,
spit shined shoes and
wearing an
"A" section
baseball cap.

.

I will
spend eight hours
electronically spying
on Russians,
East Germans and
Pollocks.

Strategically placed
speakers play

outside music,
all around our
40,000 square foot
radio shack.
Navy and
Air Force personnel
work inside.

Two German
spies on
far dirt dyke
stand with an
electronic dish,
listening for anything
except music.
It is hopeless,
music drowns out
all other sounds, but
spies keep trying to
gather information.
German,
part-time or
full-time spies,
sell information
bits or pieces to
Russian agents.

I pass security,
showing ID,
satisfying visual test,
then walk down
two corridors,
heading towards
"R" branch spaces.
It's my last
"Midnight" watch.
Tomorrow I have

three days off to
relax and sleep.

I work
2-2-2,
Eve, Day
Mid watches.
Two watches,
back to back,
make a six-day
work schedule.

I play basketball
whenever possible.
Sometimes
getting only a
few sleep hours
between watches.
I don't mind
sacrificing
sleep for basketball.

4:00 P.M. Tuesday May 11, 1965

I am slowly
warming up for
another section
basketball game.
I play on three
different teams,
probably playing a
ninety games season.

We infrequently
practice,
lack coaching,
shoot quickly and

run simple
offenses, but
we're fairly good.
I would say
small college
team equal.

Basketball is
competitive with many
teams contending.
Supervisors ask,
"Do you play
Basketball?"
They seek parity
when assigning
new people to
various branches and
sections.

They assigned
me to an already
good "A" section team.
My team is happy,
learning that I'm a
Hoosier,
thinking all
Indiana boys
know basketball and
shoot well.
I don't disappoint.

8:00 P.M. Wednesday May 12, 1965

I see some
friends at an
NCO club
round table

waving, but
I head directly to a
slot machine to
my right,
selecting favorite
end one.

I insert two
German marks,
quickly pull
waiting handle.
Nothing matches.
I insert two
quarters,
confidently pulling;
friends watch
knowing strategy.

My machine
rolls quietly and
soon shows
three cherries.
I win
four quarters,
drink two
fifty cent
beers with
my friends and
leave.

My evening
entertainment
cheaply cost
me but fifty cents.
I do this
frequently.
Two beers are

my limit,
except on
rare occasions.

I used to go
downtown, but
quit that drinking,
fighting thing.
I only go there
occasionally now.
It's too violent and
rough downtown.

There're possibly
forty segregated
Army, Navy,
Air Force and
German bars
downtown.
I'm a time
traveler and a
film maker, and
don't fit in
down there anymore.
It's a different world
down there.
I'm a different person
up here.
Maturity seems to be
seeping into
my learning,
recording and
remembering head.

8:00 A.M. Thursday, May 13, 1965

Downtown

Petula Clark is singing
"Downtown" in my head and
she soon provokes movies of
downtown Bremerhaven that
mind flash as if I'm on stage
gazing into projector light.

o

I see old Mercedes
taxicabs speeding
up and down narrow
cobblestone streets.
Mercedes autos are
expensive, but
mechanically reliable and
seem to last forever.
I walk a lot and
use cable cars,
trains and buses, and
occasionally a taxicab.
It's hard to believe
I haven't driven in
nearly two years.

I used to frequent
bars and clubs
downtown.
There must be
fifteen or twenty
just for American
military people.
Every service has

its own staked out
property with
invitation only.
And then there are
German bars.

Fighting is a sport
downtown.
I don't go there
much anymore.
It's a dangerous
unique place.
I don't think
Petula Clark
would approve.
Therefore, when
I hear her singing,
"Downtown,"
mixed feelings and
diverse movies
come to mind,
remembering good,
bad and ugly.
I grew up much
from time spent and
not spent downtown.

Peenemunda

Now quiet Peenemunda
Lies north on a
Baltic Sea shore as if
Somehow forgetting
Own history,
Remembering not that
It ignorantly helped
Germans send
V-1 and V-2 rockets
Towards fearful
England during WWII.

Sub-pins yet remain
Here in quiet
Bremerhaven.
Germans pulled
Silent submarines
Into four feet thick
Concrete protective
Bunkers that remain
In good condition as if
Constructed yesterday.
Once vigilant
Concrete turrets
Filled with deadly
Antiaircraft guns also
Remain, but are sadly
Crumbling from
Allied bombing as if
Twenty was two hundred
Enduring years ago.
War seems long ago, but
Time fools and

Drains memories from
Mind's seeking restoration.
Now it's ever spicy
Cold War seasoning
On an invented nuclear
Sandwich of deadly
Meat between
WWII and Korea that
scares everyone.

Vibrant downtown prospers
Seemingly untouched by
Allied bombing,
Certainly unlike yet rebuilding
Devastated Bremen.
There are two Bremens;
Old part, not bombed,
Historically standing and
New part, bombed and
Reveling in reconstruction hope.
I can only imagine
Bremerhaven and
Bremen then, for
I have only limiting
1964-66 movies
In my head now.

Traveling Europe

John Dace is
asking to join me
on a two-week trip
through southern Europe.
I say, "Ok, but
it will be a
cultural thing not a
party thing."
He agrees that
we will not get drunk
every night and
sleep all day.
His life is mostly
drinking, working and
sleeping,
executed in that
order.
He agrees to
my rules and promises to
practice discipline.

9:00 A.M. Monday, June 6, 1965

We are on a train
heading south
towards Paris.
We are excited.
I have traveled
Germany,
been on a few
basketball trips, but
have not traveled to
other countries.

I am sure
Dace is an
alcoholic.
NSGA usually
drums out
alcoholics, but
he is yet with us.
Drunks are a
security risk.
He must be
good at his job.
He is "T" branch,
Teletype.

2:00 A.M. Tuesday, June 7, 1965

I am laying
face up,
looking at
ceiling tiles in a
Paris hotel,
thinking I am
finally seeing a
world only
dreamed of, and
I am a
long way from
our farm
in Indiana.
Dace and
I take in many
familiar sites.
Eifel Tower,
Louvre and
River Seine.
We eat out,
drink little and

sleep well.
Paris is a place to
spend three days to
see surface stuff, but
it requires
three weeks to
know it well.
We elect to
see surface stuff.

2:00 A.M. Sunday, June 13, 1965

Barcelona, Spain is
wonderful.
I love this place.
Of course,
we must see a
bull fight.
Dace says
killing a bull
won't bother
him, but
when it happens,
it bothers
him greatly.
Of course,
growing up on a
farm prepared me for
such things.
I am not
affected.
I marvel at
matador
athletic ability.
We witness
number three
best in Spain.

He is great,
bull horns coming
close,
cape gracefully
fanning and
sword skillfully
penetrating.
There are some
gruesome parts, and
it seems cruel, but
in final analysis;
it is bull fighting,
it is understood
life and death.

2:00 A.M. Sunday, June 13, 1965

We wake
looking out over a
Mediterranean Sea
inlet and bay from a
hotel window
in southern France.
We stay in that
small town a
few days,
getting to know
real French people,
drinking a licorice
tasting drink that
is clear, but turns yellow
when adding water.
I think it is called
"pastis."
Many Frenchmen at
more than one bar are
yet grateful for

American liberation of
France.
We buy few drinks.

2:00 A.M. Sunday, June 20, 1965

We continue to
travel up through
France,
passing through
Switzerland,
heading towards
Germany.
It takes more than
twenty-four hours to
get home.
Trains here are
slow, but on time.
I am reminded of
trains behind
my house at home.
I always wished to
ride them, but
never did.
We drink wine and
eat cheese with locals
on trains and in
little bars.
We are drinking
more than
I planned.
I think, however,
it's ok.
I am gaining an
education in
many ways here
through time and

distance, through
self-discipline and
control.

2:00 A.M. Sunday, June 22, 1965

We are getting off
our train in
Bremerhaven.
Dace decides to
go downtown.
He is thirsty,
having had little to
drink for two weeks.
He admits to
having a
great time and is
grateful to me, but
he just needs a
few beers.
He goes
downtown and
remains there for
two days.
I recall all that
I have seen,
playing films of
Europe in
my head.
I think
I shall never forget
Spain,
my favorite
country,
wishing to return
someday.

Outward and Inward

Outward earthly following
concerns me through
work and play.

Inward spiritual clarifying
secretly concerns me a
great deal more.

I am miraculously finding
myself through thought,
meditation and writing.

Thought is composing
chosen ideas to promote honorable
choices and decisions.

Meditation is discovering
what is spiritually given to each
from a higher source.

Writing is describing
purpose for constructing life with
logical components.

o

Experience formed illusion as mind
captured time and movies confirmed
space as heavenly soul collected life.

Chapter XII

AUGUST 1965

Sunday	Monday	Tuesday	Wednesday	Thursday	Friday	Saturday
1	2	3	4	5	6	7
8	9	10	11	12	13	14
15	16	17	18	19	20	21
22	23	24	25	26	27	28
29	30	31				

www.PrintableCalendar.com

Contrasting Worlds

I feel good for
I have just intercepted
my first Russian nuclear
submarine message.

I am officially spying
on Russian ships.
I add another
puzzle piece to a
worldwide intelligence
enigma.

War Games

I am aboard an
old C-119 two-engine
prop airplane,
flying out of an
Reykjavik, Iceland airport.
It is vibrating and
straining to carry
heavy cargo.
We are low altitude
flying over North Sea
target area.

We are in
civilian clothing with
no military ID,
pretending to be
weathermen,
just in case
we're shot down or
crash and
won't be
considered spies.
It's 16:00
Zulu time,
we're making a
final pass before
heading back to
Iceland.

Several
different NSGA
branches are aboard.
I'm "R,"

"O" is
nearby and a
linguist is
sitting beside me.
There are at least
thirty of us,
all crammed together
among electronic
spying equipment.
Our cargo plane
hardly gets off a
small Reykjavik
runway because of
too much weight.
It is straining from
burdensome weight.

We're observing and
electronically spying on
Baltic Sea Russian and
Polish Navy war games.
We've been here for
three long days,
getting hazardous
duty pay,
putting in long hours.
It's interesting, but a
bit scary.
We're now making
last pass.
I look out a
small window,
passing over a
Russian ship
close enough to see
"Ruskie" sailors
waving hello.

It's all fun and
games out here,
same as back in
my Bremerhaven
radio shack or
National Security Agency
in Washington D.C.
Russians know
our mission like
we know their mission.
It's a gathering and
learning military spy
love affair between
U.S. and Russia.
It's who collects best
military information
most accurately, that
counts each and
every day worldwide.
It's a deadly sport
we play and
on surface,
it seems ridiculous, but
in final analysis,
deadly cold war is
no game.

3:00 A.M. Sunday, January 2, 1966

New Targets

I vividly see my
radio shack full of
young men
secretly capturing
Russian, Polish and
East German
secret messages.
Mind projector
plays sophisticated
organic movies of
previous experiences.

I am anxiously
waiting to hear
RUNSUB 101105.
It's a target designation
for a Russian Navy
nuclear submarine.

I watch clock hands,
clicking precious seconds.
I know target sending
signal time and
frequency.
I roll two Super
Heterodyne receiver
frequency knobs back and
forth across
expected frequency.
Miles of antennas
search for my elusive target while
radio receivers wait a
particular musical sound.

Tick, tick
continues clock,
radio static hampers
slightly as
I anxiously await
my counterpart.

3:30 A.M. Sunday, January 2, 1966

I finally hear perfectly
spaced "V"
Morse code sounds
sent by a
Russian radio operator
on my targeted
nuclear submarine
North Sea located,
Pacific heading.
I hear "dit dit dit da—
dit dit dit da" and
nervously wait for
international call letters.

Instantly I hear
sending of
International Morse code, a
hello or "CQ," to all
ships and stations,
"DE RUNB" and
then a
radio operator
flies into a
twenty second message,
giving encrypted
location and
brief details,
then a

final "AR" or
good-bye and
all falls silent except
environmental static.

3:31 A.M. Sunday, January 2, 1966

I lean back in
dim lighted
radio shack,
letting anxiety fade.
I feel good for
I have just intercepted
my first Russian nuclear
submarine message.
I am officially spying
on Russian ships.
I add another
puzzle piece to a
worldwide intelligence
enigma.
Naval Security
Group Activity,
working for National
Security Agency, has made
our world safer.
I have made
our world safer in
my own little way.

Another piece of
innocence is
chipped away and
yet a considerable
innocent chunk of that
little naive boy remains.
I also have much more to

experience, learn and
be accountable.
I go back to searching
night sky for signals,
secrets and enemies.
Oh well, "c'est la vie—
c'est la guerre," I say.
It is a "Cold War" night
on a cold North Sea.

o

I am afraid
nothing changes.
Sticks and stones
do break bones.
Words start wars and
men speak foul words.
Man battles himself in
timeless collide and
will never change.

Gone Wrong

I am in new
expanded spaces as
changing procedures
bring Marines and
Air Force
personnel aboard.
There are forty CTs,
blue dungaree and
denim dressed,
all working in a
straight-line with
radios humming,
headset placed,
Communist spying.
Old Underwood
typewriters printing,
minds gathering
precious results
on six ply
colored paper.

My Commander is
passageway
walking towards
me with an
entourage of six
officers following.
I've never seen
him before.
He never comes
down here.
They are moving fast.
Two officers fan out,

moving towards
section leaders.
Three chiefs pass
behind me,
whispering.
Chiefs are real Navy.
They run things,
get thing done,
do heavy lifting.
Officers direct,
chiefs work.
I pay attention to
everyone and
everything and
soon realize
something big is
happening.

Encrypted messages are
flying through our
radios and typewriters.
I intercept many myself,
unable to read them,
only plain text
Polish Shipping
can be read, but
I don't read or
speak Polish.
Some messages are
decoded here,
most are decoded at
NSA,
Washington DC.
My intercepts,
however, are
different today,
sent faster,

dit and da
Morse code
numbers and letters
not well spaced.

I hear
Morse code
"V" sounds through
my headphones,
then more code, then
three buzzing
sound bursts,
separated by a
few seconds.
It's a scrambled
message sent by a
special machine
from a Ruskie
Baltic Sea ship.
A final Morse
code "AR" and
it's all over.
"Keep it sharp
men," my
section leader says.
I can hear
excitement in
his voice.
A rumor
begins to float,
seemingly real, but
unconfirmed, that a
sortie jet fighter
secretly flew into
East Germany,
then into Russia and
was shot down.

We monitor
ships, airplanes and
missile facilities.
When missile
doors open,
air craft scramble and
ships maneuver,
we listen in and a
pilot turns back
just in time,
heading home safely.
It's a game
both sides play.
Navy and Air Force
monitor all action,
learning their
preparedness and
response time.
This time,
our pilot didn't
turn around in time.
A Russians missile
probably
shot him down.
No one reports
something like this
in newspapers.
I understand
Russia lost one
two years ago,
same scenario,
except we
shot him down.

All is now quiet.
I will never know

anything except rumor.
No one will tell
what happened.
I guess only a few
know big secrets or
truth about
things like this.
"Need to know
basis," they preach.
"Top Secret,"
they insist.
My movies are
only about
my NSGA spaces.
Anything outside of
here is strictly
based on my
imagination.

o

Way down below where
night lines toiled and held
me close and kept me as a
ship wishing to draw sail,
tied with hemp and strength,
I asked who would provide a
way to set me free, know my
haunting needs and desires
night after night?
I spoke, but no one heard.
I was a pitiful ship, wishing to sail,
dead in water and betrayed.

Saying Good-bye

It is tough
saying good-bye
when happy
about leaving.
It is just like
when
I left
my family
two years ago.
These guys are
family also.
Vinnie, Al, Joe,
Henry, Ron and
Tillman come to
moving
picture mind.
My list of
pals goes on.
Communication
Technicians without
glory, without
recognition,
keeping secrets,
keeping peace.
Who will
remember what
happened at
Naval Security
Group Activity
Bremerhaven,
Germany
except those
who served here?

Oh, I play those
movies yet
in my head.
I see those faces,
those spaces and
those graces.
They meld
now into
mind lights,
heights and
delights.
I can only leave
written records.
I wish
I could show
my movies to
you now.
Good-byes
sort emotions into
good, bad and
ugly of
family, friends and
foes.

Coming Home

I see Statue of Liberty
gallantly standing below
my Boeing 707 wingtip,
causing heart flutters,
deeper breaths while
mind movie camera
in vivid color
records everything

I see her high
torch standing,
welcoming me home.
I sincerely feel
hundred percent
American,
knowing German
heritage, but
deliberately feel
American
first and last.

I've been liberty
fighting in
own quiet way,
Cold War spying,
warm peace seeking.
I am not
same person as
when leaving
these shores.
McGuire
Air Force Base is
long ago.

I left a boy,
returning a man.

I know self
importance and
worldly
unimportance.
I know
goal setting and
affirmed
fatherly advice.
I've slowly
matured,
found discipline
through time and
freedom.
I'm more
controlled,
believing in
own luck.
Advice and
discipline yet
encourage a
boy to conquer
manhood.

I yet seek self
understanding and
life placement.
"Know Thyself,"
I whisper,
remembering
Socrates and
his lingering advice
shared with me
so many years ago.

Time and Distance

I venture onward in
Mindless poetic rhetoric,
Writing and dreaming again,
Movie making still.

Movie projector whines,
History is alive in
Head, mind and soul as if
Europe a dream.

o

Into morning I stretch
To grasp future, but
Like a filthy window,
Wisdom hesitates clarity.

Eyes and mind are
Exhausted as
Stars gaze back,
Lighting fantasy paths.

I willingly dream
Everything is possible and
Nothing has little
Cogent dispelling power.

Enlightenment shouts
Recognizable names and
Movie fame shimmers
Brilliant history.

I see truth,
Justice, equality as
Journey fearlessly moves
Towards life learning.

I courageously shift,
Staying awake and
Leisurely walk into
God's sun lit grace.

Gallant wisdom and
Awareness
I magnificently gain in
Life's inevitable soul.

Understanding is
Self knowing through
Unique dreams and
Gathered altered beliefs.

I am able to reach far,
Accomplishing much as
Morning provides another
Moving picture day.

o

I see home farm,
Long driveway,
Big white farm house
Seeking my attention.

I return a man,
Many ways liberated.
I hug my father,
First time in life.

Maturity is a
complicated thing
attained through
ingenuous forces.

I have discipline,
Strength and resolve,
Being a man
Comes naturally.

9:00 A.M. Sunday, March 20, 1966

I face wind with
watering eyes,
squinting to see
maple trees dancing.
Fall amber and
brown are
long gone and
forgotten.
No one can
remember
leaf death and
decay.
Only spring
comes to mind
with its
glorious rebirth and
eternal living
renewal.
One tree allows
ten thousand
green leaves to
murmur and
together they
create a loud
musical drone.

Then ten more
lush trees
together play a
graceful
thriving wind
symphony.
I sway and
flow to a
moody melody,
slowly dancing
my way home.
I close eyes,
open mind and
gather peace
within
my grasping
soul.
It is a nice
place to be.
I shall not
enter heaven with
any better
disposition.

CONCLUSION

I yet play
moving
organic pictures in
my earthly head.
Someday
film maker and
theater will
also become
organic.
My movies
shall become
spiritual jewels
preserved by a
collecting soul
forever and ever.

o

Dust of body,
movie of mind,
spirit of soul,
I sought your
innocence
again and again.

ABOUT AUTHOR

Phillip Reisner has been seeing movies and writing poetry in his head all while growing up on a mid-western farm and venturing out to all parts of the world. He learned efficiency of thought, action and description from his father who was a man of few words. Phillip tries to write with word efficiency, sometimes letting even one word speak meaningfully alone. His poetry tells stories and professes philosophy with simple words.

Phillip lives in Lafayette, Indiana, not so far from where he began becoming aware of life and self, and where he began creating the movies he describes in his latest book, "I See Movies in My Head."